# HASHIMOTO
# DIET
## FOR BEGINNERS

*A Cookbook with 100 Quick, Easy, and Delicious Recipes for Thyroid Healing and a 30-Day Meal Plan*

SARAH GRACE MORGAN

# CONTENTS

# HEALTHY
# EATING

# INTRODUCTION

Meet Sarah, a vibrant and energetic woman in her early thirties. Throughout her life, Sarah had always been known for her enthusiasm and zest for adventure. She loved exploring new places, trying out different cuisines, and living life to the fullest. However, in recent years, Sarah started feeling a sense of exhaustion that seemed to linger, no matter how much rest she got.

Initially, she brushed it off as the result of her busy lifestyle, thinking she just needed a vacation to recharge. But as time went on, Sarah began experiencing other troubling symptoms. She struggled with unexplained weight gain, her hair became dry and brittle, and she felt an overwhelming sense of sadness and irritability.

Concerned, Sarah visited her doctor, who ran several tests. The results revealed that Sarah had Hashimoto's disease, an autoimmune condition that affects the thyroid gland.

Her doctor explained that Hashimoto's occurs when the immune system mistakenly attacks the thyroid, leading to an underactive thyroid or hypothyroidism. This diagnosis left Sarah feeling overwhelmed and uncertain about her future.

She had always taken her health for granted, and the idea of a chronic illness seemed like an insurmountable obstacle. However, Sarah's determination and her desire to regain control of her life led her on a journey to discover the power of a well-balanced diet in managing Hashimoto's.

With a newfound determination, Sarah immersed herself in research, seeking out information on the connection between food and autoimmune diseases. She quickly learned that making dietary changes could have a significant impact on her symptoms and overall well-being.

Sarah discovered that certain foods could trigger inflammation in her body and worsen Hashimoto's symptoms. She also learned that her diet could support her thyroid function and reduce the autoimmune response. Armed with this knowledge, she embarked on a mission to overhaul her eating habits.

She started by eliminating processed foods, refined sugars, and gluten from her diet. Instead, Sarah focused on incorporating nutrient-dense ingredients that supported her thyroid and reduced inflammation. She loaded her plate with colorful fruits and vegetables, lean proteins like fish and poultry, and healthy fats from avocados, nuts, and olive oil. Sarah found that these whole foods not only nourished her body but also gave her a renewed sense of vitality and energy.

As Sarah continued to explore and refine her diet, she started developing delicious and easy-to-make recipes that not only supported her health but also satisfied her taste buds. She experimented with flavorful spices and herbs, creating dishes that were both nourishing and exciting to eat. From hearty salads to comforting soups and creative grain-free alternatives, Sarah's culinary creations proved that eating well didn't mean sacrificing taste.

Throughout her journey, Sarah encountered others who were struggling with similar health challenges. She realized that she wasn't alone in her battle against Hashimoto's, and many others could benefit from her experiences and the knowledge she had gained.

Motivated by the desire to help others facing similar challenges, Sarah decided to write "Hashimoto's Diet for Beginners: A Cookbook with 100 Quick, Easy, and Delicious Recipes for Thyroid Healing and a 30-Day Meal Plan. "This book encompasses her journey, delves into the scientific aspects of Hashimoto's disease, and presents an extensive selection of delectable recipes carefully crafted to provide nourishment and support for individuals living with this condition."

Sarah's journey from a place of uncertainty to empowerment serves as an inspiration to anyone grappling with Hashimoto's.

Her book not only offers a roadmap to managing the condition but also provides a delicious and accessible way to regain control over one's health. With Sarah's guidance, readers can embark on their culinary adventure, finding joy and healing through the power of food.

# CHAPTER 1

## What is Hashimoto's Disease?

Hashimoto's disease is an autoimmune disorder that primarily affects the thyroid gland, a small butterfly-shaped organ located in the neck. In this condition, the immune system mistakenly attacks the thyroid, leading to inflammation and impairment of its function. As a result, the thyroid may become underactive, leading to a decrease in the production of essential hormones.

This chronic condition affects millions of people worldwide, predominantly women. While the exact cause of Hashimoto's disease remains unclear, a combination of genetic predisposition and environmental triggers is believed to play a role. Factors such as family history, certain infections, and excessive iodine intake have been linked to the development of the disease.

The symptoms of Hashimoto's disease can vary widely and may be subtle in the early stages. Fatigue, weight gain, dry skin, and hair loss are common complaints. Individuals may also experience muscle aches, joint pain, depression, and a slowed heart rate. As the disease progresses, symptoms can become more pronounced and have a significant impact on daily life.

Diagnosing Hashimoto's disease involves a combination of medical history evaluation, physical examination, and blood tests to measure thyroid hormone levels and detect specific antibodies associated with the condition. Once diagnosed, treatment typically focuses on hormone replacement therapy, which involves taking synthetic thyroid hormones to compensate for the decreased hormone production.

While medication is crucial in managing the disease, lifestyle modifications, including dietary changes, play a vital role in supporting overall health and minimizing symptoms. Adapting a well-balanced diet rich in nutrient-dense foods, minimizing stress levels, optimizing sleep patterns, and incorporating regular physical activity can have a positive impact on thyroid function and overall well-being.

## Symptoms of Hashimoto's Disease

Hashimoto's disease manifests through a range of symptoms that can vary from person to person. While some individuals may experience mild manifestations, others may encounter more pronounced effects.

Fatigue is a common symptom, with individuals often feeling tired, sluggish, and lacking energy. Weight gain, despite efforts to maintain a healthy lifestyle, is another prevalent complaint. Other physical symptoms include dry and pale skin, brittle nails, and hair loss.

Emotional well-being may also be affected, as individuals with Hashimoto's disease often experience mood swings, depression, and difficulty concentrating. Additionally, muscle aches, joint pain, and stiffness can be present, making daily activities challenging. Women may notice irregular menstrual cycles or heavier periods. It's important to note that not all individuals will experience every symptom, and the severity may vary.

The onset of Hashimoto's disease can be gradual, making it challenging to attribute these symptoms solely to the condition. It is crucial to consult a healthcare professional for a comprehensive evaluation and accurate diagnosis. Recognizing and understanding the symptoms can empower individuals to seek appropriate medical attention and access the necessary treatment and management strategies.

## Causes of Hashimoto's Disease

The precise causes of Hashimoto's disease, an autoimmune condition affecting the thyroid gland, are not fully understood. However, researchers believe that a combination of genetic and environmental factors contributes to the development of this condition.

Genetics plays a role in predisposing individuals to autoimmune disorders like Hashimoto's disease. Having a family history of thyroid conditions or autoimmune diseases increases the likelihood of developing the condition. Certain gene variants associated with immune system regulation and thyroid function have been identified as potential risk factors.

Environmental triggers also play a significant role in the onset of Hashimoto's disease. Viral or bacterial infections, particularly those affecting the respiratory or gastrointestinal systems, have been linked to triggering an autoimmune response in susceptible individuals. Additionally, exposure to high levels of iodine, typically from medications or supplements, can potentially induce or worsen the condition in some individuals.

Other factors that may contribute to the development of Hashimoto's disease include hormonal imbalances, such as postpartum changes in women after childbirth, and chronic stress, which can impact immune system function and increase the risk of autoimmune disorders.

It's important to note that while these factors are associated with Hashimoto's disease, they do not guarantee its development. The interplay between genetic susceptibility and environmental triggers is complex and can vary from person to person.

Understanding the potential causes of Hashimoto's disease can help individuals gain insights into their risk factors and take proactive steps toward managing the condition.

By working closely with healthcare professionals and adopting a comprehensive approach that includes medication, lifestyle modifications, and stress management techniques, individuals can effectively navigate the challenges posed by Hashimoto's disease and improve their overall well-being.

## Treatments for Hashimoto's Disease

Hashimoto's disease, an autoimmune condition that affects the thyroid gland, requires a comprehensive treatment approach to manage symptoms and optimize thyroid function. The primary goal of treatment is to restore hormone balance and alleviate the associated symptoms.

Treatment options for Hashimoto's disease typically include hormone replacement therapy, medication management, lifestyle modifications, and the potential incorporation of supplements.

Hormone replacement therapy involves the use of synthetic thyroid hormones to compensate for the reduced hormone production caused by the disease. This therapy aims to normalize thyroid hormone levels in the body, alleviating symptoms like fatigue, weight gain, and mood changes. It requires regular monitoring and adjustment to ensure optimal hormone levels.

Medication management may involve the use of additional medications to address specific symptoms or related conditions. For example, individuals with co-existing depression or anxiety may benefit from antidepressant or anti-anxiety medications.

It is important to work closely with a healthcare professional to determine the appropriate medications and dosages for each individual.

In addition to medication, lifestyle modifications play a crucial role in managing Hashimoto's disease. A well-balanced diet that focuses on nutrient-dense foods can support thyroid health and overall well-being. Stress management techniques, regular exercise, and adequate sleep are also vital in optimizing immune function and reducing symptom severity.

Supplements, such as selenium, vitamin D, and omega-3 fatty acids, may be recommended in some cases to support thyroid function and reduce inflammation.

However, it is essential to consult with a healthcare professional before starting any supplements to ensure safety and effectiveness.

## The Importance of Diet and Lifestyle Changes for Hashimoto's Disease

In the management of Hashimoto's disease, adopting a healthy diet and making lifestyle changes can play a pivotal role in supporting thyroid health, alleviating symptoms, and promoting overall well-being.

While medication is essential, dietary and lifestyle modifications can complement medical treatments and enhance their effectiveness.

A well-balanced diet rich in nutrient-dense foods is crucial for individuals with Hashimoto's disease. Including plenty of fruits, vegetables, whole grains, lean proteins, and healthy fats can provide essential vitamins, minerals, and antioxidants that support immune function and reduce inflammation. Moreover, avoiding processed foods, excessive sugar, and refined carbohydrates can help stabilize blood sugar levels and manage weight, which are common challenges for those with Hashimoto's disease.

Reducing stress levels is paramount, as stress can exacerbate symptoms and impact thyroid function.

Engaging in stress-reducing activities such as yoga, meditation, deep breathing exercises, or engaging hobbies can help manage stress levels and promote emotional well-being. Regular exercise is beneficial for individuals with Hashimoto's disease, as it can improve mood, increase energy levels, and support overall health.

Engaging in activities such as walking, swimming, or low-impact exercises can boost metabolism, aid in weight management, and enhance overall fitness levels.

Optimizing sleep is also crucial for individuals with Hashimoto's disease. Creating a sleep routine, ensuring a comfortable sleep environment, and prioritizing sufficient rest can contribute to hormone regulation, immune function, and overall wellness.

While dietary and lifestyle changes cannot cure Hashimoto's disease, they can significantly impact symptom management, hormone balance, and overall quality of life. Individuals need to work closely with healthcare professionals, such as dietitians and endocrinologists, to develop a personalized plan that addresses their specific needs and optimizes their well-being.

# Foods to Avoid with Hashimoto's Disease

1. **Gluten**: Many individuals with Hashimoto's disease have gluten intolerance or celiac disease, which can exacerbate inflammation and autoimmune responses. Therefore, it is advisable to limit or eliminate gluten-containing foods from your diet.
2. **Soy**: Soy contains compounds called goitrogens that can interfere with thyroid hormone production. It is recommended to limit soy consumption, especially in its unfermented form.
3. **Cruciferous Vegetables**: Vegetables like broccoli, cauliflower, cabbage, and Brussels sprouts contain goitrogens. While these vegetables can still be consumed cooked in moderate amounts, it is advised to avoid consuming them raw or in large quantities.
4. **Processed Foods**: Processed foods often contain high levels of unhealthy fats, additives, preservatives, and refined sugars, which can contribute to inflammation and negatively affect overall health. It's best to minimize the intake of processed foods and focus on whole, nutrient-dense options instead.
5. **Sugary Foods and Drinks**: High sugar intake can disrupt blood sugar levels and contribute to inflammation. It is important to limit or avoid

foods and beverages with added sugars, such as sodas, candies, desserts, and sweetened beverages.

6. **Excessive Iodine**: While iodine is essential for thyroid function, excessive intake of iodine-rich foods, iodine supplements, or iodized salt can potentially worsen symptoms in some individuals with Hashimoto's disease. Consulting a healthcare professional is advised to determine individual iodine needs.

7. **Alcohol and Caffeine**: Both alcohol and caffeine can interfere with thyroid hormone production and may exacerbate symptoms such as sleep disturbances and anxiety in some individuals. It's best to consume these substances in moderation or avoid them altogether.

By being mindful of your diet and avoiding these potential trigger foods, you can help support your thyroid health and potentially reduce symptoms associated with Hashimoto's disease. Remember, everyone's body is unique, so it's important to listen to your body's signals and work closely with a healthcare professional or registered dietitian to develop a personalized dietary plan that meets your specific needs and goals.

# CHAPTER 2

## MEAL PLAN
### Week 1
Day 1:

- Breakfast: Classic Veggie Omelette
- Snack: Roasted Chickpeas
- Lunch: Quinoa Salad with Roasted Vegetables
- Dinner: Baked Salmon with Lemon-Dill Sauce
- Dessert: Chocolate Avocado Mousse

Day 2:

- Breakfast: Berry Chia Pudding
- Snack: Trail Mix with Nuts and Dried Fruits
- Lunch: Mediterranean Chickpea Salad
- Dinner: Quinoa-Stuffed Zucchini Boats
- Dessert: Berry Crumble Bars

Day 3:

- Breakfast: Spinach and Mushroom Frittata
- Snack: Veggie Sticks with Hummus
- Lunch: Caprese Stuffed Avocado
- Dinner: Chicken Stir-Fry with Vegetables
- Dessert: Banana Nut Bread

Day 4:

- Breakfast: Quinoa Breakfast Bowl
- Snack: Greek Yogurt Parfait with Granola
- Lunch: Grilled Chicken Caesar Wrap
- Dinner: Roasted Vegetable and Chickpea Quinoa Bowl
- Dessert: Coconut Chia Seed Pudding

Day 5:

- Breakfast: Green Smoothie
- Snack: Energy Balls with Dates and Nuts
- Lunch: Asian Noodle Salad
- Dinner: Lentil Curry with Brown Rice
- Dessert: Baked Apples with Cinnamon and Almonds

Day 6:

- Breakfast: Overnight Oats with Almond Butter
- Snack: Baked Kale Chips
- Lunch: Quinoa Stuffed Bell Peppers
- Dinner: Baked Turkey Meatballs with Zoodles
- Dessert: Mango Coconut Sorbet

Day 7:

- Breakfast: Avocado Toast with Smoked Salmon
- Snack: Apple Slices with Almond Butter
- Lunch: Greek Salad with Lemon Herb Chicken
- Dinner: Teriyaki Tofu Stir-Fry
- Dessert: Peanut Butter Energy Balls

# Week 2

- Breakfast: Greek Yogurt Parfait
- Snack: Mini Caprese Skewers
- Lunch: Turkey and Avocado Lettuce Wraps
- Dinner: Stuffed Bell Peppers with Quinoa and Ground Beef
- Dessert: Greek Yogurt Parfait with Fresh Fruit

Day 9:

- Breakfast: Sweet Potato Hash with Eggs
- Snack: Roasted Chickpeas
- Lunch: Mediterranean Hummus Wrap
- Dinner: Grilled Shrimp Skewers with Citrus Marinade
- Dessert: Chocolate Peanut Butter Protein Smoothie

Day 10:

- Breakfast: Blueberry Pancakes
- Snack: Trail Mix with Nuts and Dried Fruits
- Lunch: Tuna Salad Lettuce Cups
- Dinner: Sweet Potato and Black Bean Enchiladas
- Dessert: Lemon Poppy Seed Muffins

Day 11:

- Breakfast: Veggie Breakfast Burrito
- Snack: Energy Balls with Dates and Nuts
- Lunch: Black Bean and Corn Quesadillas
- Dinner: Lemon Herb Roasted Chicken with Vegetables
- Dessert: Almond Flour Blueberry Muffins

Day 12:

- Breakfast: Apple Cinnamon Overnight French Toast
- Snack: Baked Kale Chips
- Lunch: Asian Chicken Lettuce Wraps
- Dinner: Cauliflower Fried Rice with Tofu
- Dessert: Pumpkin Spice Energy Bites

Day 13:

- Breakfast: Spinach and Feta Egg Muffins
- Snack: Apple Slices with Almond Butter
- Lunch: Quinoa and Lentil Salad
- Dinner: Eggplant Parmesan with Whole Wheat Pasta
- Dessert: Mixed Berry Cobbler

Day 14:

- Breakfast: Banana Walnut Smoothie Bowl
- Snack: Greek Yogurt Parfait with Granola
- Lunch: Moroccan Spiced Chickpea Salad
- Dinner: Thai Coconut Curry with Vegetables and Tofu
- Dessert: Vanilla Chia Pudding with Fresh Berries

# Week 3

Day 15:

- Breakfast: Breakfast Quinoa with Berries
- Snack: Roasted Chickpeas
- Lunch: Quinoa Salad with Roasted Vegetables
- Dinner: Baked Salmon with Lemon-Dill Sauce
- Dessert: Chocolate Avocado Mousse

Day 16:

- Breakfast: Berry Chia Pudding
- Snack: Trail Mix with Nuts and Dried Fruits
- Lunch: Mediterranean Chickpea Salad
- Dinner: Quinoa-Stuffed Zucchini Boats
- Dessert: Berry Crumble Bars

Day 17:

- Breakfast: Spinach and Mushroom Frittata
- Snack: Veggie Sticks with Hummus
- Lunch: Caprese Stuffed Avocado
- Dinner: Chicken Stir-Fry with Vegetables
- Dessert: Banana Nut Bread

Day 18:

- Breakfast: Quinoa Breakfast Bowl
- Snack: Greek Yogurt Parfait with Granola
- Lunch: Grilled Chicken Caesar Wrap
- Dinner: Roasted Vegetable and Chickpea Quinoa Bowl
- Dessert: Coconut Chia Seed Pudding

Day 19:

- Breakfast: Green Smoothie
- Snack: Energy Balls with Dates and Nuts
- Lunch: Asian Noodle Salad
- Dinner: Lentil Curry with Brown Rice
- Dessert: Baked Apples with Cinnamon and Almonds

Day 20:

- Breakfast: Overnight Oats with Almond Butter
- Snack: Baked Kale Chips
- Lunch: Quinoa Stuffed Bell Peppers
- Dinner: Baked Turkey Meatballs with Zoodles
- Dessert: Mango Coconut Sorbet

Day 21:

- Breakfast: Avocado Toast with Smoked Salmon
- Snack: Apple Slices with Almond Butter
- Lunch: Greek Salad with Lemon Herb Chicken
- Dinner: Teriyaki Tofu Stir-Fry
- Dessert: Peanut Butter Energy Balls

# Week 4

- Breakfast: Greek Yogurt Parfait
- Snack: Mini Caprese Skewers
- Lunch: Turkey and Avocado Lettuce Wraps
- Dinner: Stuffed Bell Peppers with Quinoa and Ground Beef
- Dessert: Greek Yogurt Parfait with Fresh Fruit

- Breakfast: Sweet Potato Hash with Eggs
- Snack: Roasted Chickpeas
- Lunch: Mediterranean Hummus Wrap
- Dinner: Grilled Shrimp Skewers with Citrus Marinade
- Dessert: Chocolate Peanut Butter Protein Smoothie

- Breakfast: Blueberry Pancakes
- Snack: Trail Mix with Nuts and Dried Fruits
- Lunch: Tuna Salad Lettuce Cups
- Dinner: Sweet Potato and Black Bean Enchiladas
- Dessert: Lemon Poppy Seed Muffins

Day 25:

- Breakfast: Veggie Breakfast Burrito
- Snack: Energy Balls with Dates and Nuts
- Lunch: Black Bean and Corn Quesadillas
- Dinner: Lemon Herb Roasted Chicken with Vegetables
- Dessert: Almond Flour Blueberry Muffins

Day 26:

- Breakfast: Apple Cinnamon Overnight French Toast
- Snack: Baked Kale Chips
- Lunch: Asian Chicken Lettuce Wraps
- Dinner: Cauliflower Fried Rice with Tofu
- Dessert: Pumpkin Spice Energy Bites

Day 27:

- Breakfast: Spinach and Feta Egg Muffins
- Snack: Apple Slices with Almond Butter
- Lunch: Quinoa and Lentil Salad
- Dinner: Eggplant Parmesan with Whole Wheat Pasta
- Dessert: Mixed Berry Cobbler

Day 28:

- Breakfast: Banana Walnut Smoothie Bowl
- Snack: Greek Yogurt Parfait with Granola
- Lunch: Moroccan Spiced Chickpea Salad
- Dinner: Thai Coconut Curry with Vegetables and Tofu
- Dessert: Vanilla Chia Pudding with Fresh Berries

# Week 5

- Breakfast: Berry Chia Pudding
- Snack: Roasted Chickpeas
- Lunch: Quinoa Salad with Roasted Vegetables
- Dinner: Baked Salmon with Lemon-Dill Sauce
- Dessert: Chocolate Avocado Mousse

- Breakfast: Quinoa Breakfast Bowl
- Snack: Trail Mix with Nuts and Dried Fruits
- Lunch: Mediterranean Chickpea Salad
- Dinner: Quinoa-Stuffed Zucchini Boats
- Dessert: Berry Crumble Bars

# Gluten-Free 7-Day Meal Plan

Day 1:

- Breakfast: Berry Chia Pudding
- Snack: Roasted Chickpeas
- Lunch: Quinoa Salad with Roasted Vegetables
- Dinner: Baked Lemon Herb Chicken with Quinoa
- Dessert: Chocolate Avocado Mousse

Day 2:

- Breakfast: Spinach and Mushroom Frittata
- Snack: Trail Mix with Nuts and Dried Fruits
- Lunch: Cauliflower Pizza Crust (toppings of choice)
- Dinner: Zucchini Noodles with Pesto
- Dessert: Berry Crumble Bars

Day 3:

- Breakfast: Quinoa Breakfast Bowl
- Snack: Veggie Sticks with Hummus
- Lunch: Mediterranean Chickpea Salad
- Dinner: Shrimp Stir-Fry with Rice Noodles
- Dessert: Banana Nut Bread

Day 4:

- Breakfast: Green Smoothie
- Snack: Greek Yogurt Parfait with Granola
- Lunch: Mexican Stuffed Bell Peppers with Brown Rice
- Dinner: Baked Lemon Herb Chicken with Quinoa
- Dessert: Coconut Chia Seed Pudding

Day 5:

- Breakfast: Overnight Oats with Almond Butter
- Snack: Energy Balls with Dates and Nuts
- Lunch: Greek Salad with Lemon Herb Chicken
- Dinner: Cauliflower Fried Rice with Tofu
- Dessert: Baked Apples with Cinnamon and Almonds

Day 6:

- Breakfast: Avocado Toast with Smoked Salmon
- Snack: Mini Caprese Skewers
- Lunch: Quinoa Stuffed Bell Peppers
- Dinner: Zucchini Noodles with Pesto
- Dessert: Mango Coconut Sorbet

Day 7:

- Breakfast: Breakfast Quinoa with Berries
- Snack: Apple Slices with Almond Butter
- Lunch: Mediterranean Chickpea Salad
- Dinner: Baked Lemon Herb Chicken with Quinoa
- Dessert: Peanut Butter Energy Balls

## Dairy-Free 7-Day Meal Plan

Day 1:

- Breakfast: Vegan Spinach and Mushroom Frittata

- Snack: Roasted Chickpeas
- Lunch: Quinoa Salad with Roasted Vegetables
- Dinner: Lentil Curry with Brown Rice
- Dessert: Dairy-Free Chocolate Avocado Mousse

## Day 2:

- Breakfast: Coconut Milk Smoothie
- Snack: Trail Mix with Nuts and Dried Fruits
- Lunch: Mediterranean Chickpea Salad
- Dinner: Quinoa-Stuffed Zucchini Boats
- Dessert: Berry Crumble Bars

## Day 3:

- Breakfast: Almond Milk Chia Pudding
- Snack: Veggie Sticks with Hummus
- Lunch: Caprese Stuffed Avocado
- Dinner: Teriyaki Tofu Stir-Fry
- Dessert: Banana Nut Bread

## Day 4:

- Breakfast: Classic Veggie Omelette (without dairy)
- Snack: Energy Balls with Dates and Nuts
- Lunch: Greek Salad with Lemon Herb Chicken (without dairy)
- Dinner: Roasted Vegetable and Chickpea Quinoa Bowl with Tahini Dressing
- Dessert: Coconut Chia Seed Pudding

## Day 5:

- Breakfast: Green Smoothie
- Snack: Greek Yogurt Parfait with Granola (using dairy-free yogurt)
- Lunch: Mediterranean Hummus Wrap
- Dinner: Cauliflower Fried Rice with Tofu
- Dessert: Baked Apples with Cinnamon and Almonds

Day 6:

- Breakfast: Overnight Oats with Almond Butter
- Snack: Mini Caprese Skewers (using dairy-free cheese alternative)
- Lunch: Quinoa Stuffed Bell Peppers
- Dinner: Thai Coconut Curry with Vegetables and Tofu
- Dessert: Mango Coconut Sorbet

Day 7:

- Breakfast: Berry Chia Pudding
- Snack: Apple Slices with Almond Butter
- Lunch: Quinoa and Lentil Salad
- Dinner: Quinoa-Stuffed Portobello Mushrooms
- Dessert: Peanut Butter Energy Balls

## Pescetarian 7-Day Meal Plan
Day 1:

- Breakfast: Classic Veggie Omelette

- Snack: Roasted Chickpeas
- Lunch: Quinoa Salad with Roasted Vegetables
- Dinner: Grilled Salmon with Lemon-Dill Sauce
- Dessert: Chocolate Avocado Mousse

## Day 2:

- Breakfast: Berry Chia Pudding
- Snack: Trail Mix with Nuts and Dried Fruits
- Lunch: Tuna Poke Bowl
- Dinner: Quinoa-Stuffed Zucchini Boats
- Dessert: Berry Crumble Bars

## Day 3:

- Breakfast: Avocado Toast with Smoked Salmon
- Snack: Veggie Sticks with Hummus
- Lunch: Mediterranean Chickpea Salad
- Dinner: Garlic Shrimp Stir-Fry with Vegetables
- Dessert: Coconut Chia Seed Pudding

## Day 4:

- Breakfast: Overnight Oats with Almond Butter
- Snack: Energy Balls with Dates and Nuts
- Lunch: Caprese Stuffed Avocado
- Dinner: Baked Cod with Mediterranean Salsa
- Dessert: Baked Apples with Cinnamon and Almonds

## Day 5:

- Breakfast: Quinoa Breakfast Bowl

- Snack: Greek Yogurt Parfait with Fresh Fruit
- Lunch: Asian Noodle Salad
- Dinner: Zucchini and Salmon Cakes
- Dessert: Mango Coconut Sorbet

## Day 6:

- Breakfast: Spinach and Mushroom Frittata
- Snack: Mini Caprese Skewers
- Lunch: Quinoa and Lentil Salad
- Dinner: Greek-Style Grilled Fish Skewers
- Dessert: Peanut Butter Energy Balls

## Day 7:

- Breakfast: Sweet Potato Hash with Eggs
- Snack: Apple Slices with Almond Butter
- Lunch: Moroccan Spiced Chickpea Salad
- Dinner: Shrimp and Quinoa Stuffed Bell Peppers
- Dessert: Vanilla Chia Pudding with Fresh Berries

# Vegan 7-Day Meal Plan

Day 1:

- Breakfast: Berry Chia Pudding
- Snack: Roasted Chickpeas
- Lunch: Mediterranean Chickpea Salad
- Dinner: Chickpea Curry with Coconut Milk
- Dessert: Chocolate Avocado Mousse

Day 2:

- Breakfast: Green Smoothie
- Snack: Trail Mix with Nuts and Dried Fruits
- Lunch: Quinoa Stuffed Bell Peppers
- Dinner: Vegan Lentil Bolognese with Zucchini Noodles
- Dessert: Berry Crumble Bars

Day 3:

- Breakfast: Avocado Toast with Smoked Salmon (using vegan smoked salmon alternative)
- Snack: Veggie Sticks with Hummus
- Lunch: Mediterranean Hummus Wrap
- Dinner: Roasted Vegetable Quinoa Salad
- Dessert: Coconut Chia Seed Pudding

Day 4:

- Breakfast: Overnight Oats with Almond Butter
- Snack: Energy Balls with Dates and Nuts
- Lunch: Asian Noodle Salad
- Dinner: Vegan Black Bean Burgers
- Dessert: Baked Apples with Cinnamon and Almonds

Day 5:

- Breakfast: Classic Veggie Omelette (vegan version using plant-based eggs)
- Snack: Greek Yogurt Parfait with Fresh Fruit (using dairy-free yogurt)
- Lunch: Quinoa and Lentil Salad
- Dinner: Sweet Potato and Chickpea Coconut Curry
- Dessert: Mango Coconut Sorbet

Day 6:

- Breakfast: Banana Walnut Smoothie Bowl
- Snack: Mini Caprese Skewers (using vegan cheese alternative)
- Lunch: Moroccan Spiced Chickpea Salad
- Dinner: Vegan Pad Thai with Tofu
- Dessert: Peanut Butter Energy Balls

Day 7:

- Breakfast: Breakfast Quinoa with Berries
- Snack: Apple Slices with Almond Butter
- Lunch: Caprese Stuffed Avocado (using vegan cheese alternative)
- Dinner: Quinoa-Stuffed Portobello Mushrooms
- Dessert: Vanilla Chia Pudding with Fresh Berries

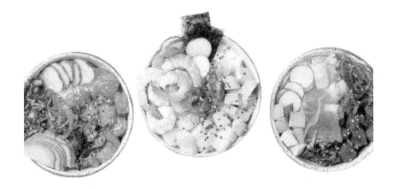

# HEALTHY
# EATING

# CHAPTER 3

## BREAKFAST RECIPES

### Classic Veggie Omelette

**Ingredients:**

- 2 eggs
- 1/4 cup chopped bell peppers
- 1/4 cup chopped onions
- 1/4 cup sliced mushrooms
- Salt and pepper to taste
- 1 tablespoon olive oil

**Estimated Time: 10 minutes**

**Nutritional Information (per serving):**

- Calories: 220
- Protein: 14g
- Fat: 15g
- Carbohydrates: 7g

**Instructions:**

1. Warm up the olive oil in a non-stick skillet on a medium heat setting.
2. Add the bell peppers, onions, and mushrooms to the skillet and sauté for 3-4 minutes until the vegetables are tender.
3. Take a bowl and whisk the eggs vigorously until well beaten. Add a pinch of salt and pepper to season the eggs.

4. Gently pour the beaten eggs over the sautéed vegetables in the skillet.
5. Cook the omelet for 2-3 minutes until the edges are set.
6. Flip the omelet and cook for an additional 2 minutes until cooked through.
7. Carefully transfer the omelet from the skillet onto a plate, and then fold it in half.
8. Serve hot and enjoy!

## Shopping List:

- Eggs - Bell peppers

- Onions - Mushrooms

- Olive oil – Salt – Pepper

Classic Veggie Omelette

# Berry Chia Pudding

## Ingredients:

- 1/4 cup chia seeds
- 1 cup almond milk (or any non-dairy milk)
- 1 tablespoon maple syrup (optional)
- 1/2 cup mixed berries (strawberries, blueberries, raspberries)

**Estimated Time: 5 minutes (plus refrigeration time)**

**Nutritional Information (per serving):**

- Calories: 180
- Protein: 5g
- Fat: 9g
- Carbohydrates: 22g

## Instructions:

1. In a bowl, combine the chia seeds, almond milk, and maple syrup (if using). Stir well to combine.
2. Allow the mixture to rest for approximately 5 minutes, giving it time to settle. Afterward, give it a gentle stir to ensure that clumping is avoided.
3. Place a cover or lid on the bowl, then refrigerate it for a minimum of 2 hours, or ideally overnight. This duration allows the chia seeds to absorb the liquid and create a thickened consistency.
4. After the chia pudding has reached the desired thickness, give it a thorough stir to ensure an even consistency throughout.

5. Using a spoon, carefully transfer the chia pudding into individual serving bowls or jars.
6. Top with mixed berries.
7. Serve chilled and enjoy!
8.

**Shopping List:**

- Chia seeds

- Almond milk (or any non-dairy milk)

- Maple syrup

- Mixed berries (strawberries, blueberries, raspberries)

Berry Chia Pudding

# Spinach and Mushroom Frittata

## Ingredients:

- 6 eggs
- 1 cup fresh spinach, chopped
- 1 cup sliced mushrooms
- 1/4 cup chopped onions
- 1/4 cup diced tomatoes
- Salt and pepper to taste
- 1 tablespoon olive oil

## Estimated Time: 25 minutes

## Nutritional Information (per serving):

- Calories: 220
- Protein: 16g
- Fat: 15g
- Carbohydrates: 6g

## Instructions:

1. Preheat the oven to 350°F (175°C).
2. Take a bowl and whisk the eggs until they are well beaten. Add a pinch of salt and pepper to season the eggs.
3. Place an oven-safe skillet on the stove and heat the olive oil over a medium heat setting.
4. Add the onions and mushrooms to the skillet and sauté for 3-4 minutes until the vegetables are tender.

5. Add the chopped spinach and diced tomatoes to the skillet and cook for an additional 2 minutes until the spinach wilts.
6. Pour the whisked eggs into the skillet, making sure the vegetables are evenly distributed.
7. Cook the frittata on the stovetop for 3-4 minutes until the edges start to set.
8. Transfer the skillet to the preheated oven and bake for 12-15 minutes until the frittata is set and slightly golden on top.
9. Take the skillet out of the oven and allow it to cool for a few minutes before proceeding to slice it.
10. Serve warm and enjoy!

## Shopping List:

- Eggs - Fresh spinach
- Mushrooms - Onions
- Tomatoes  - Salt
- Pepper  - Olive oil

Spinach and Mushroom Frittata

# Quinoa Breakfast Bowl

## Ingredients:

- 1/2 cup cooked quinoa
- 1/4 cup almond milk (or any non-dairy milk)
- 1 tablespoon honey or maple syrup
- 1/4 cup mixed berries (strawberries, blueberries, raspberries)
- 1 tablespoon chopped nuts (e.g., almonds, walnuts)
- 1 tablespoon unsweetened coconut flakes

**Estimated Time: 10 minutes**

**Nutritional Information (per serving):** Calories: 220 - Protein: 6g - Fat: 7g- Carbohydrates: 35g

## Instructions:

1. In a bowl, combine the cooked quinoa, almond milk, and honey or maple syrup. Stir well to combine.
2. Top the quinoa mixture with mixed berries, chopped nuts, and unsweetened coconut flakes.
3. Serve at room temperature or chilled and enjoy!

**Shopping List:** - Quinoa

- Almond milk (or any non-dairy milk)
- Honey or maple syrup
- Mixed berries (strawberries, blueberries, raspberries)
- Chopped nuts (e.g., almonds, walnuts)
- Unsweetened coconut flakes

# Green Smoothie:

## Ingredients:

- 1 ripe banana
- 1 cup fresh spinach
- 1/2 cup almond milk (or any non-dairy milk)
- 1/2 cup Greek yogurt
- 1 tablespoon honey or maple syrup
- 1/2 cup ice cubes

## Estimated Time: 5 minutes

## Nutritional Information (per serving):

- Calories: 160
- Protein: 10g
- Fat: 2g
- Carbohydrates: 30g

## Instructions:

1. Place all the ingredients in a blender.
2. Blend on high speed until smooth and creamy.
3. If desired, add more almond milk for a thinner consistency or more ice cubes for a thicker smoothie.
4. Pour into a glass and serve immediately.

## Shopping List:

- Ripe banana, Greek yogurt
- Fresh spinach, Ice cubes, Honey, or maple syrup
- Almond milk (or any non-dairy milk)

## Overnight Oats with Almond Butter
### Ingredients:

- 1/2 cup rolled oats
- 1/2 cup almond milk (or any non-dairy milk)
- 1 tablespoon almond butter
- 1 tablespoon maple syrup (optional)
- 1/4 cup mixed berries (strawberries, blueberries, raspberries)
- 1 tablespoon chopped nuts (e.g., almonds, walnuts)

**Estimated Time: 5 minutes (plus overnight refrigeration)**

**Nutritional Information (per serving):**

- Calories: 320
- Protein: 8g
- Fat: 12g
- Carbohydrates: 45g

### Instructions:

1. In a jar or container, combine the rolled oats, almond milk, almond butter, and maple syrup (if using). Stir well to combine.
2. Cover the jar or container and refrigerate overnight or for at least 4 hours to allow the oats to soften and absorb the liquid.

3. In the morning, thoroughly stir the oats to ensure they are well-mixed.
4. Top with mixed berries and chopped nuts.
5. Enjoy the overnight oats chilled!


## Shopping List:

- Rolled oats
- Almond milk (or any non-dairy milk)
- Almond butter
- Maple syrup
- Mixed berries (strawberries, blueberries, raspberries)
- Chopped nuts (e.g., almonds, walnuts)
-

Overnight Oats with Almond Butter

# Avocado Toast with Smoked Salmon

**Ingredients:**

- 2 slices whole wheat bread, toasted
- 1 ripe avocado
- Juice of 1/2 lemon
- Salt and pepper to taste
- 2-3 ounces smoked salmon
- Fresh dill or chives for garnish (optional)

**Estimated Time: 10 minutes**

**Nutritional Information (per serving):**

- Calories: 380 - Protein: 20g
- Fat: 18g - Carbohydrates: 34g

**Instructions:**

1. Take a bowl and combine the ripe avocado with lemon juice, salt, and pepper. Mash the ingredients together until well blended.
2. Take the toasted bread slices and spread the mashed avocado mixture evenly onto each slice.
3. Top each slice with smoked salmon.
4. If desired, add a final touch to your dish by garnishing it with fresh dill or chives.
5. Serve the avocado toast immediately and enjoy!

**Shopping List:**

- Whole wheat bread- Ripe avocado- Lemon- Salt- Pepper- Smoked salmon- Fresh dill or chives (optional)

# Greek Yogurt Parfait

**Ingredients:**

- 1 cup Greek yogurt
- 1 tablespoon honey or maple syrup
- 1/4 cup granola
- 1/4 cup mixed berries (strawberries, blueberries, raspberries)
- 1 tablespoon chopped nuts (e.g., almonds, walnuts)

**Estimated Time: 5 minutes**

**Nutritional Information (per serving):** Calories: 280

- Protein: 20g - Fat: 10g -Carbohydrates: 30g

**Instructions:**

1. In a glass or bowl, layer Greek yogurt, honey or maple syrup, granola, mixed berries, and chopped nuts.
2. Repeat the layers until all the ingredients are used, ending with a sprinkle of granola, berries, and nuts on top.
3. Serve the Greek yogurt parfait immediately or refrigerate until ready to eat.

**Shopping List:**- Greek yogurt - Honey or maple syrup

- Granola - Mixed berries (strawberries, blueberries, raspberries)

- Chopped nuts (e.g., almonds, walnuts)

# Sweet Potato Hash with Eggs

## Ingredients:

- 1 large sweet potato, peeled and diced
- 1/2 red bell pepper, diced
- 1/2 yellow bell pepper, diced
- 1/2 small red onion, diced
- 2 tablespoons olive oil
- 1 teaspoon paprika
- 1/2 teaspoon garlic powder
- Salt and pepper to taste
- 2 eggs
- Fresh parsley or cilantro for garnish (optional)

## Estimated Time: 20 minutes

## Nutritional Information (per serving):

- Calories: 380
- Protein: 12g
- Fat: 20g
- Carbohydrates: 40g

## Instructions:

1. Warm up the olive oil in a large skillet on a medium heat setting.
2. Add the sweet potato, bell peppers, and red onion to the skillet. Sprinkle the mixture with paprika, garlic powder, salt, and pepper, ensuring that the seasonings are evenly distributed. Stir to combine.

3. Cook for about 15 minutes, stirring occasionally, until the sweet potato is tender and slightly crispy.
4. While the sweet potato hash is cooking, prepare the eggs to your liking (e.g., fried, poached, scrambled).
5. Serve the sweet potato hash with the cooked eggs on top.
6. If desired, add a final touch to your dish by garnishing it with fresh parsley or cilantro, adding a touch of vibrant flavor and visual appeal.
7. Enjoy the sweet potato hash with eggs!

## Shopping List:

- Sweet potato
- Red bell pepper - Yellow bell pepper
- Red onion - Olive oil
- Paprika
- Garlic powder - Salt
- Pepper - Eggs
- Fresh parsley or cilantro (optional)

# Blueberry Pancakes

## Ingredients:

- 1 cup all-purpose flour
- 2 tablespoons sugar
- 1 teaspoon baking powder
- 1/2 teaspoon baking soda
- 1/4 teaspoon salt
- 3/4 cup buttermilk
- 1/4 cup almond milk (or any non-dairy milk)
- 1 large egg
- 2 tablespoons unsalted butter, melted
- 1/2 teaspoon vanilla extract
- 1 cup fresh blueberries
- Maple syrup for serving

**Estimated Time: 20 minutes**

**Nutritional Information (per serving, without maple syrup):**

- Calories: 300
- Protein: 7g
- Fat: 8g
- Carbohydrates: 50g

## Instructions:

1. Take a large bowl and vigorously whisk together the flour, sugar, baking powder, baking soda, and salt until they are well combined.

2. In a separate bowl, whisk together the buttermilk, almond milk, egg, melted butter, and vanilla extract.
3. Carefully pour the wet ingredients into the bowl containing the dry ingredients. Stir the mixture gently until the ingredients are just combined, being careful not to overmix. Do not overmix.
4. Gently fold in the fresh blueberries.
5. Preheat a non-stick skillet or griddle over a medium heat setting and lightly grease the surface with cooking spray or butter.
6. Using a measuring cup or ladle, pour approximately 1/4 cup of batter onto the skillet for each pancake, spacing them out to allow room for spreading.
7. Cook for 2-3 minutes on one side until bubbles form on the surface, then flip and cook for an additional 1-2 minutes until golden brown.
8. Repeat with the remaining batter.
9. Serve the blueberry pancakes warm with maple syrup.

**Shopping List:**

- All-purpose flour
- Sugar
- Baking powder
- Baking soda, Salt
- Buttermilk
- Almond milk (or any non-dairy milk)
- Egg - Unsalted butter- Vanilla extract
- Fresh blueberries - Maple syrup

## Veggie Breakfast Burrito

**Ingredients:**

- 2 large tortillas (whole wheat or gluten-free)
- 4 large eggs
- 1/4 cup diced bell peppers (any color)
- 1/4 cup diced tomatoes
- 1/4 cup diced red onion
- 1/4 cup shredded cheddar cheese (or any cheese of your choice)
- Salt and pepper to taste
- Salsa or hot sauce for serving

**Estimated Time: 15 minutes**

**Nutritional Information (per serving):**

- Calories: 360
- Protein: 18g
- Fat: 15g
- Carbohydrates: 38g

**Instructions:**

1. In a bowl, whisk the eggs together with a pinch of salt and pepper.
2. Heat a non-stick skillet over medium heat and lightly coat with cooking spray or a drizzle of oil.
3. Add the diced bell peppers, tomatoes, and red onion to the skillet. Cook for 2-3 minutes until slightly softened.

4. Pour the whisked eggs into the skillet, combining them with the sautéed vegetables. Cook the mixture, stirring occasionally, until the eggs are scrambled and thoroughly cooked. Cook, stirring occasionally, until the eggs are scrambled and fully cooked.
5. Warm the tortillas in a microwave or on a stovetop griddle.
6. Divide the scrambled eggs and vegetable mixture evenly between the tortillas.
7. Generously sprinkle shredded cheese over the cooked eggs, allowing it to melt and create a delicious cheesy layer on top.
8. Roll up the tortillas tightly, making sure to tuck in the sides as you go, creating a compact and secure wrap.
9. Serve the veggie breakfast burritos with salsa or hot sauce on the side.

**Shopping List:**

- Tortillas (whole wheat or gluten-free)
- Eggs
- Bell peppers (any color)
- Tomatoes - Red onion
- Shredded cheddar cheese (or any cheese of your choice)
- Salt, Pepper, Salsa, or hot sauce

# Apple Cinnamon Overnight French Toast

**Ingredients:**

- 4 slices of bread (preferably day-old bread)
- 2 large eggs
- 1/2 cup almond milk (or any non-dairy milk)
- 1 tablespoon maple syrup
- 1/2 teaspoon vanilla extract
- 1 apple, thinly sliced
- 1 tablespoon melted butter
- 1 teaspoon ground cinnamon
- Maple syrup or powdered sugar for serving

**Estimated Time: 30 minutes (plus overnight refrigeration)**

**Nutritional Information (per serving, without additional toppings):**

- Calories: 280
- Protein: 9g
- Fat: 11g
- Carbohydrates: 36g

**Instructions:**

1. Apply a light coating of cooking spray or butter to grease the baking dish, ensuring that the surface is well coated and the ingredients won't stick.
2. Place the bread slices in a single layer, ensuring they are evenly arranged, within the baking dish.

3. In a bowl, whisk together the eggs, almond milk, maple syrup, and vanilla extract.
4. Pour the egg mixture evenly over the bread slices, ensuring they are fully coated.
5. Arrange the apple slices on top of the bread.
6. In a separate bowl, mix melted butter and ground cinnamon.
7. Drizzle the cinnamon butter mixture over the apple slices.
8. Cover the baking dish with plastic wrap, ensuring it is tightly sealed, and then refrigerate overnight or for a minimum of 6 hours. This allows the flavors to meld and the bread to absorb the custard mixture.
9. Preheat the oven to 350°F (175°C).
10. Remove the plastic wrap from the baking dish and bake the French toast for 20-25 minutes until golden and the bread is fully cooked.
11. Serve the apple cinnamon overnight French toast warm with maple syrup or powdered sugar.

**Shopping List:**

- Bread (preferably day-old bread)
- Eggs
- Almond milk (or any non-dairy milk)
- Maple syrup
- Vanilla extract
- Apple - Butter
- Ground cinnamon
- Maple syrup or powdered sugar

# Spinach and Feta Egg Muffins

## Ingredients:

- 6 large eggs
- 1/4 cup milk
- 1 cup fresh spinach, chopped
- 1/4 cup crumbled feta cheese
- 1/4 cup diced tomatoes
- 1/4 cup diced red onion
- Salt and pepper to taste

**Estimated Time: 25 minutes**

**Nutritional Information (per serving):**

- Calories: 120
- Protein: 10g
- Fat: 8g
- Carbohydrates: 2g

## Instructions:

1. Preheat the oven to 350°F (175°C) and grease a muffin tin with cooking spray or line it with paper liners.
2. Take a bowl and vigorously whisk together the eggs and milk until they are well combined. Season with salt and pepper.
3. Stir in the chopped spinach, crumbled feta cheese, diced tomatoes, and diced red onion into the egg mixture.

4. Pour the egg mixture evenly into the prepared muffin tin, filling each cup about 3/4 full.
5. Bake for 15-18 minutes or until the egg muffins are set and slightly golden on top.
6. Take the dish out of the oven and allow the contents to cool for a brief period before serving. This will prevent any potential burns and ensure a more enjoyable eating experience.
7. Serve the spinach and feta egg muffins as a grab-and-go breakfast option.

**Shopping List:**

- Eggs- Milk
- Fresh spinach
- Feta cheese
- Tomatoes
- Red onion
- Salt - Pepper

Spinach and Feta Egg Muffins

# Banana Walnut Smoothie Bowl

## Ingredients:

- 2 ripe bananas, frozen
- 1/2 cup almond milk (or any non-dairy milk)
- 1 tablespoon almond butter (or any nut butter)
- 1/4 cup Greek yogurt (optional, for added creaminess)
- 2 tablespoons rolled oats
- 1 tablespoon honey or maple syrup (optional, for sweetness)
- 1/4 cup chopped walnuts
- Fresh fruit and additional toppings of your choice (e.g., berries, sliced banana, shredded coconut, chia seeds)

**Estimated Time: 10 minutes**

**Nutritional Information (per serving, without additional toppings):**

- Calories: 380
- Protein: 9g
- Fat: 18g
- Carbohydrates: 51g

## Instructions:

1. In a blender, combine the frozen bananas, almond milk, almond butter, Greek yogurt (if using), rolled oats, and honey or maple syrup (if desired).
2. Blend until smooth and creamy.

3. Pour the smoothie into a bowl.
4. Top with chopped walnuts and any additional toppings of your choice, such as fresh fruit, shredded coconut, or chia seeds.
5. Serve the banana walnut smoothie bowl immediately.

**Shopping List:**

- Ripe bananas
- Almond milk (or any non-dairy milk)
- Almond butter (or any nut butter)
- Greek yogurt (optional)
- Rolled oats
- Honey or maple syrup (optional)
- Chopped walnuts
- Fresh fruit and additional toppings of your choice (e.g., berries, shredded coconut, chia seeds)
-

Banana Walnut Smoothie Bowl

# Breakfast Quinoa with Berries

## Ingredients:

- 1 cup cooked quinoa
- 1/2 cup almond milk (or any non-dairy milk)
- 1 tablespoon honey or maple syrup (optional, for sweetness)
- 1/2 teaspoon vanilla extract
- 1 cup mixed berries (e.g., strawberries, blueberries, raspberries)
- 2 tablespoons chopped nuts (e.g., almonds, walnuts, pecans)
- Fresh mint leaves for garnish (optional)

**Estimated Time: 10 minutes**

**Nutritional Information (per serving):**

- Calories: 280
- Protein: 8g
- Fat: 8g
- Carbohydrates: 45g

## Instructions:

1. In a saucepan, heat the cooked quinoa and almond milk over medium heat.
2. Stir in the honey or maple syrup (if desired) and vanilla extract.
3. Cook, stirring occasionally, until the mixture is heated through and slightly thickened.

4. Take the skillet or pan off the heat source and allow it to cool for a short while, allowing the temperature to decrease slightly.
5. In a serving bowl, layer the quinoa mixture with the mixed berries.
6. Top with chopped nuts and garnish with fresh mint leaves (if using).
7. Serve the breakfast quinoa with berries warm or chilled.

**Shopping List:**

- Cooked quinoa
- Almond milk (or any non-dairy milk)
- Honey or maple syrup (optional)
- Vanilla extract
- Mixed berries (e.g., strawberries, blueberries, raspberries)
- Chopped nuts (e.g., almonds, walnuts, pecans)
- Fresh mint leaves (optional)

Breakfast Quinoa with Berries

# CHAPTER 4

## SNACKS RECIPES

### Roasted Chickpeas

**Ingredients:**

- 1 can (15 ounces) chickpeas (garbanzo beans)
- 1 tablespoon olive oil
- 1 teaspoon paprika
- 1/2 teaspoon garlic powder
- 1/2 teaspoon cumin
- Salt to taste

**Estimated Time: 35 minutes**

**Nutritional Information (per serving):**

- Calories: 120
- Protein: 6g
- Fat: 4g
- Carbohydrates: 16g

**Instructions:**

1. Preheat the oven to 400°F (200°C). Drain and rinse the chickpeas.
2. Pat the chickpeas dry with a paper towel and remove any loose skins.
3. In a bowl, toss the chickpeas with olive oil, paprika, garlic powder, cumin, and salt until well coated.

4. Arrange the chickpeas in a single, even layer on a baking sheet, ensuring that they are well-spaced and not overcrowded.
5. Roast the chickpeas in the preheated oven for 25-30 minutes, shaking the pan halfway through, until they are crispy and golden brown.
6. Remove from the oven and let the roasted chickpeas cool before serving.

**Shopping List:**

- Canned chickpeas
- Olive oil
- Paprika
- Garlic powder
- Cumin
- Salt

Roasted Chickpeas

# Trail Mix with Nuts and Dried Fruits

## Ingredients:

- 1 cup mixed nuts (such as almonds, walnuts, and cashews)
- 1/2 cup dried fruits (such as raisins, cranberries, apricots)
- 1/4 cup seeds (such as pumpkin seeds, or sunflower seeds)
- 1/4 cup dark chocolate chips or chunks (optional)

## Estimated Time: 5 minutes

## Nutritional Information (per serving):

- Calories: 200
- Protein: 6g
- Fat: 14g
- Carbohydrates: 16g

## Instructions:

1. In a bowl, combine the mixed nuts, dried fruits, seeds, and dark chocolate chips (if using).
2. Toss the ingredients together until well-mixed.
3. Carefully transfer the trail mix into an airtight container, ensuring that it is sealed tightly to maintain freshness during storage.
4. Serve the trail mix as a convenient and healthy snack option.

**Shopping List:**

- Mixed nuts (almonds, walnuts, cashews)

- Dried fruits (raisins, cranberries, apricots)

- Seeds (pumpkin seeds, sunflower seeds)

- Dark chocolate chips or chunks (optional)

Trail Mix with Nuts and Dried Fruits

## Veggie Sticks with Hummus

**Ingredients:**

- Assorted vegetables (carrots, celery, bell peppers, cucumber, cherry tomatoes, etc.)
- Hummus for dipping

**Estimated Time: 10 minutes**

**Instructions:**

1. Wash and cut the assorted vegetables into sticks or bite-sized pieces.
2. Arrange the vegetable sticks on a platter or individual serving plates.
3. Serve the veggie sticks with hummus as a nutritious and refreshing snack.

**Shopping List:**

- Assorted vegetables (carrots, celery, bell peppers, cucumber, cherry tomatoes, etc.)
- Hummus

Veggie Sticks with Hummus

# Greek Yogurt Parfait with Granola

**Ingredients:**

- 1 cup Greek yogurt (dairy-free if desired)
- 1/2 cup granola (gluten-free if desired)
- Fresh berries or sliced fruits of your choice (such as strawberries, blueberries, and bananas)
- Honey or maple syrup (optional, for added sweetness)

**Estimated Time: 5 minutes**

**Nutritional Information (per serving):**

- Calories: 300
- Protein: 15g
- Fat: 10g
- Carbohydrates: 40g

**Instructions:**

1. In a glass or bowl, layer Greek yogurt, granola, and fresh berries or sliced fruits.
2. Repeat the layers until all the ingredients are used, finishing with a layer of granola and fruits on top.
3. If desired, drizzle the prepared dish with honey or maple syrup to add a touch of natural sweetness.
4. Serve the Greek yogurt parfait immediately as a satisfying and wholesome snack.

**Shopping List:**

- Greek yogurt (dairy-free if desired)
- Granola (gluten-free if desired)
- Fresh berries or sliced fruits (strawberries, blueberries, bananas)
- Honey or maple syrup (optional)

**Greek Yogurt Parfait with Granola**

-

# Energy Balls with Dates and Nuts

## Ingredients:

- 1 cup pitted dates
- 1 cup nuts (such as almonds, cashews, or a mixture)
- 2 tablespoons nut butter (such as almond butter or peanut butter)
- 2 tablespoons unsweetened cocoa powder or shredded coconut (for coating, optional)

**Estimated Time: 15 minutes**

## Instructions:

1. Place the pitted dates, nuts, and nut butter in a food processor.
2. Blend or process the ingredients together until they reach a sticky dough-like consistency, ensuring that all the ingredients are well combined.
3. Using a scoop or spoon, take small portions of the dough and roll them between your palms to form bite-sized balls. Continue this process until all the dough has been shaped into balls.
4. If desired, roll the energy balls in unsweetened cocoa powder or shredded coconut for coating.
5. Transfer the energy balls into an airtight container and place them in the refrigerator. Allow them to chill for a minimum of 1 hour before serving. This

will help the balls firm up and enhance their texture.

6. Enjoy the energy balls as a quick and nourishing snack.

## Shopping List:

- Pitted dates
- Nuts (almonds, cashews, or a mixture)
- Nut butter (almond butter or peanut butter)
- Unsweetened cocoa powder or shredded coconut (optional, for coating)

Energy Balls with Dates and Nuts

# Baked Kale Chips

## Ingredients:

- 1 bunch of kale
- 1 tablespoon olive oil
- Salt and pepper to taste

**Estimated Time**: 20 minutes **Shopping List:** - Kale

## Nutritional Information (per serving):

- Calories: 50
- Protein: 2g
- Fat: 3g
- Carbohydrates: 6g

## Instructions:

1. Preheat the oven to 350°F (175°C). Line a baking sheet with parchment paper.
2. Thoroughly wash the kale leaves under running water to remove any dirt or debris. After washing, ensure to dry them completely, either by patting them gently with a clean towel or by using a salad spinner.
3. Trim off and discard the tough stems from the kale leaves. Tear the leaves into bite-sized pieces, suitable for the desired texture and presentation of your dish.
4. In a bowl, toss the kale leaves with olive oil, salt, and pepper until well coated.

5. Arrange the kale leaves in a single layer on the baking sheet that has been prepared for this purpose. Ensure that the leaves are evenly spaced and not overlapping to facilitate even baking.
6. Bake in the preheated oven for 12-15 minutes, or until the kale leaves are crispy and slightly browned.
7. Remove from the oven and let the kale chips cool before serving.

Baked Kale Chip

# Apple Slices with Almond Butter

**Ingredients:**

- Apples (any variety)
- Almond butter or any nut butter of your choice

**Estimated Time: 5 minutes**

**Instructions:**

1. Wash and slice the apples into thin rounds or wedges.
2. Arrange the apple slices on a plate or serving dish.
3. Serve the apple slices with a side of almond butter or any nut butter for dipping.
4. Enjoy the apple slices with almond butter as a healthy and satisfying snack.

**Shopping List:**

- Apples
- Almond butter or any nut butter of your choice

Apple Slices with Almond Butter

# Mini Caprese Skewers

## Ingredients:

- Cherry or grape tomatoes
- Fresh mozzarella cheese balls
- Fresh basil leaves
- Balsamic glaze or balsamic reduction (optional)

## Estimated Time: 10 minutes

## Instructions:

1. Wash the cherry or grape tomatoes and pat them dry.
2. Thread a tomato, a fresh mozzarella cheese ball, and a fresh basil leaf onto a small skewer or toothpick.
3. Continue to repeat the process, using the same steps, until all of the ingredients have been utilized. This ensures that each batch of the dish is prepared consistently and thoroughly.
4. Arrange the mini Caprese skewers on a serving platter.
5. Drizzle with balsamic glaze or balsamic reduction, if desired, for added flavor.
6. Serve the mini Caprese skewers as a delightful and appetizing snack.

**Shopping List:** Cherry or grape tomatoes

Fresh mozzarella cheese balls - Fresh basil leaves

- Balsamic glaze or balsamic reduction (optional)

Mini Caprese Skewers

Greek Yogurt Parfait

# CHAPTER 5

## LUNCH RECIPES

### Quinoa Salad with Roasted Vegetables

- **Ingredients:**

    - 1 cup quinoa
    - Assorted vegetables (e.g., bell peppers, zucchini, eggplant)
    - Olive oil
    - Salt and pepper
    - Fresh herbs (e.g., parsley, basil) for garnish

- **Instructions:**

1. Preheat the oven to 400°F (200°C).
2. Prepare the quinoa by following the instructions on the package. Once cooked, set it aside to cool or use it as directed in your recipe.
3. Cut the assorted vegetables into bite-sized pieces and place them on a baking sheet.
4. Drizzle a generous amount of olive oil over the vegetables, ensuring they are evenly coated. Season with salt and pepper to enhance the flavors.
5. Roast the vegetables in the preheated oven for about 20 minutes or until tender.
6. In a large mixing bowl, gently combine the cooked quinoa and roasted vegetables, ensuring that they are evenly distributed throughout the mixture.
7. Garnish with fresh herbs.

8. Serve warm or chilled.

**Estimated time: 30 minutes**

**Nutritional information (per serving):**

- Calories: 250
- Protein: 8g
- Fat: 10g
- Carbohydrates: 35g

**- Shopping list:**

quinoa, assorted vegetables, olive oil, fresh herbs

**Qui no a Salad with Roasted Vegetables**

# Mediterranean Chickpea Salad

## Ingredients:

- 1 can chickpeas, drained and rinsed
- Cucumber, diced
- Cherry tomatoes, halved
- Red onion, thinly sliced
- Kalamata olives, pitted and halved
- Feta cheese, crumbled (optional)
- Lemon juice
- Olive oil
- Fresh herbs (e.g., parsley, mint) for garnish

## Instructions:

1. In a large mixing bowl, combine the chickpeas, cucumber, cherry tomatoes, red onion, and kalamata olives.
2. If using, sprinkle crumbled feta cheese over the salad.
3. Drizzle lemon juice and olive oil over the ingredients.
4. Toss gently to combine.
5. Garnish with fresh herbs.
6. Serve chilled

## Estimated time: 15 minutes

## Nutritional information (per serving):

- Calories: 220
- Protein: 9g

- Fat: 8g
- Carbohydrates: 30g

**Shopping list:**

Chickpeas, cucumber, cherry tomatoes, red onion, kalamata olives, feta cheese (optional), lemon juice, olive oil, fresh herbs

Mediterranean Chickpea Salad

# Caprese Stuffed Avocado

**Ingredients:**

- Ripe avocados
- Cherry tomatoes, halved
- Fresh mozzarella cheese, diced
- Fresh basil leaves, torn
- Balsamic glaze
- Salt and pepper

**Instructions:**

1. Using a knife, carefully cut the avocados in half lengthwise. Then, remove the pits by gently scooping them out with a spoon.
2. Scoop out some of the flesh from each avocado half to create a hollow space.
3. In a mixing bowl, combine the cherry tomatoes, mozzarella cheese, and torn basil leaves.
4. Season the mixture with salt and pepper, adjusting the amount to your taste preferences. Add a little at a time, tasting as you go, until you achieve the desired level of seasoning.
5. Take each avocado half and fill it with the tomato and mozzarella mixture, ensuring that each avocado half is generously filled.
6. Drizzle balsamic glaze over the stuffed avocados.
7. Serve as is or refrigerate for a while before serving.

**Estimated time: 10 minutes**

**Nutritional information (per serving):**

- Calories: 180
- Protein: 6g
- Fat: 14g
- Carbohydrates: 9g

**Shopping list:**

Avocados, cherry tomatoes, fresh mozzarella cheese, fresh basil leaves, balsamic glaze

Caprese Stuffed Avocado

# Grilled Chicken Caesar Wrap

## Ingredients:

- Grilled chicken breast, sliced
- Whole wheat tortillas
- Romaine lettuce, shredded
- Caesar dressing
- Parmesan cheese, grated

## Instructions:

1. Place a whole wheat tortilla flat on a clean surface.
2. Place some sliced grilled chicken breast in the center of the tortilla.
3. Top with shredded romaine lettuce.
4. Drizzle Caesar dressing over the ingredients.
5. Sprinkle-grated Parmesan cheese on top.
6. Roll up the tortilla tightly to form a wrap.
7. Cut the wrap in half if desired.
8. Serve immediately or wrap in foil for later use.

**Estimated time: 15 minutes**

**Nutritional information (per serving):**

Calories: 320, Protein: 25g, Fat: 12g, Carbohydrates: 26g

- **Shopping list:** grilled chicken breast, whole wheat tortillas, romaine lettuce, Caesar dressing, Parmesan cheese

# Asian Noodle Salad

## Ingredients:

- Rice noodles
- Bell peppers, thinly sliced
- Carrots, julienned
- Cucumber, thinly sliced
- Red cabbage, shredded
- Green onions, sliced
- Fresh cilantro, chopped
- Sesame seeds
- Soy sauce
- Rice vinegar
- Lime juice
- Honey or maple syrup (optional)
- Sesame oil
- Garlic, minced
- Ginger, grated

## Instructions:

1. Cook rice noodles as per package instructions.
2. In a large mixing bowl, combine the cooked rice noodles, bell peppers, carrots, cucumber, red cabbage, green onions, and fresh cilantro.
3. In a small bowl, whisk together soy sauce, rice vinegar, lime juice, honey or maple syrup (optional), sesame oil, minced garlic, and grated ginger to make the dressing.
4. Pour dressing over noodles and vegetables.

5. Toss gently to coat all the ingredients.
6. Sprinkle sesame seeds on top for garnish.
7. Serve chilled.

**Estimated time: 20 minutes**

**Nutritional information (per serving):**

- Calories: 290
- Protein: 8g
- Fat: 5g
- Carbohydrates: 53g

**Shopping list:** rice noodles, bell peppers, carrots, cucumber, red cabbage, green onions, fresh cilantro, sesame seeds, soy sauce, rice vinegar, lime juice, honey or maple syrup, sesame oil, garlic, ginger

Asian Noodle Salad

# Quinoa Stuffed Bell Peppers

## Ingredients:

- Bell peppers (any color)
- Cooked quinoa
- Black beans, rinsed and drained
- Corn kernels
- Onion, diced
- Garlic, minced
- Cumin
- Chili powder
- Salt and pepper
- Shredded cheese (optional)
- Fresh cilantro, chopped (for garnish)

## Instructions:

1. Preheat the oven to 375°F (190°C).
2. Cut off pepper tops and remove seeds/membranes.
3. In a mixing bowl, combine cooked quinoa, black beans, corn kernels, diced onion, minced garlic, cumin, chili powder, salt, and pepper.
4. Spoon quinoa mixture into peppers, filling to the top.
5. Put stuffed peppers in baking dish, cover with foil.
6. Bake for 25-30 minutes until peppers are tender.
7. Remove the foil and sprinkle shredded cheese on top if desired.
8. Return to the oven and bake for an additional 5 minutes, or until the cheese is melted and bubbly.

9. Garnish with chopped fresh cilantro before serving.

**Estimated time: 45 minutes**

**Nutritional information (per serving):**

- Calories: 220
- Protein: 9g
- Fat: 4g
- Carbohydrates: 40g

**Shopping list**: bell peppers, cooked quinoa, black beans, corn kernels, onion, garlic, cumin, chili powder, shredded cheese (optional), fresh cilantro

## Greek Salad with Lemon Herb Chicken
**Ingredients:**

- Boneless, skinless chicken breasts

- Lemon juice
- Olive oil
- Garlic, minced
- Dried oregano
- Salt and pepper
- Romaine lettuce, chopped
- Cucumber, diced
- Cherry tomatoes, halved
- Kalamata olives, pitted and sliced
- Red onion, thinly sliced
- Feta cheese, crumbled
- Greek dressing

**Instructions:**

1. In a small bowl, combine lemon juice, olive oil, minced garlic, dried oregano, salt, and pepper to make the marinade.
2. Put chicken breasts in a resealable bag, and pour marinade over. Seal the bag and refrigerate for 30 minutes to 4 hours.
3. Preheat the grill/grill pan over medium heat.
4. Grill the marinated chicken breasts for about 6-8 minutes per side, or until cooked through. Allow a few minutes for them to rest, then slice.
5. In a large salad bowl, combine chopped romaine lettuce, diced cucumber, halved cherry tomatoes, sliced Kalamata olives, thinly sliced red onion, and crumbled feta cheese.

6. Drizzle Greek dressing over the salad and toss to coat.
7. Top the salad with the sliced lemon herb chicken.
8. Serve immediately.

**Estimated time: 40 minutes**

**Nutritional information (per serving):**

- Calories: 350
- Protein: 32g
- Fat: 18g
- Carbohydrates: 15g

**Shopping list:** boneless, skinless chicken breasts, lemon juice, olive oil, garlic,

Dried oregano, romaine lettuce, cucumber, cherry tomatoes,

Kalamata olives, red onion, feta cheese, Greek dressing

# Caprese Quinoa Bowl

**Ingredients:**

- Cooked quinoa
- Cherry tomatoes, halved
- Fresh mozzarella cheese, cubed
- Fresh basil leaves, torn
- Balsamic glaze
- Olive oil
- Salt and pepper

**Instructions:**

1. In a bowl, combine cooked quinoa, halved cherry tomatoes, cubed fresh mozzarella cheese, and torn basil leaves.
2. Drizzle with balsamic glaze and olive oil.
3. Season with salt and pepper to taste.
4. Toss everything together until well combined.
5. Serve the caprese quinoa salad in bowls.

**Estimated time: 15 minutes**

**Nutritional information (per serving):**

- Calories: 280    - Protein: 12g

- Fat: 12g    - Carbohydrates: 30g

**Shopping list:** cooked quinoa, cherry tomatoes, fresh mozzarella cheese, fresh basil leaves, balsamic glaze, olive oil

# Turkey and Avocado Lettuce Wraps

**Ingredients:**

- Ground turkey
- Onion, finely chopped
- Garlic, minced
- Ground cumin
- Chili powder
- Salt and pepper
- Butter lettuce leaves
- Avocado, sliced
- Tomato, diced
- Greek yogurt or sour cream (optional, for topping)
- Lime wedges (for serving)

**Instructions:**

1. Heat a large skillet over medium heat and add ground turkey, chopped onion, minced garlic, ground cumin, chili powder, salt, and pepper.
2. Cook until the turkey is browned and cooked through, breaking it up into crumbles with a spatula.
3. Place lettuce leaves on a platter.
4. Spoon the cooked turkey mixture onto each lettuce leaf.
5. Top with sliced avocado and diced tomato.
6. If desired, drizzle with Greek yogurt or sour cream.

7. Serve the lettuce wraps with lime wedges on the side.

**Estimated time: 25 minutes**

**Nutritional information (per serving):**

- Calories: 220

- Protein: 20g

- Fat: 12g

- Carbohydrates: 9g

**Shopping list:** ground turkey, onion, garlic, ground cumin, chili powder, butter lettuce leaves, avocado, tomato, Greek yogurt or sour cream, lime

Turkey and Avocado Lettuce Wraps

# Mediterranean Hummus Wrap

## Ingredients:

- Whole wheat or gluten-free wrap
- Hummus
- Cucumber, sliced
- Tomato, sliced
- Red onion, thinly sliced
- Kalamata olives, pitted and sliced
- Feta cheese, crumbled
- Fresh parsley, chopped
- Lemon juice
- Olive oil
- Salt and pepper

## Instructions:

1. Lay the whole wheat or gluten-free wrap on a clean surface.
2. Spread a generous amount of hummus over the wrap.
3. Layer cucumber slices, tomato slices, thinly sliced red onion, Kalamata olives, crumbled feta cheese, and chopped fresh parsley over the hummus.
4. Drizzle with lemon juice and olive oil.
5. Season with salt and pepper to taste.
6. Roll wrap tightly, tucking sides.
7. Cut the wrap in half and serve.

**Estimated time: 10 minutes**

## Nutritional information (per serving):

- Calories: 300
- Protein: 12g
- Fat: 10g
- Carbohydrates: 40g

**Shopping list:** whole wheat or gluten-free wrap, hummus, cucumber, tomato, red onion, Kalamata olives, feta cheese, fresh parsley, lemon juice, olive oil

Mediterranean Hummus Wrap

## Tuna Salad Lettuce Cups
### Ingredients:

- Canned tuna, drained
- Celery, finely chopped
- Red onion, finely chopped
- Dill pickles, finely chopped
- Mayonnaise
- Dijon mustard
- Lemon juice
- Salt and pepper
- Butter lettuce leaves
- Cherry tomatoes, halved
- Fresh dill, for garnish

### Instructions:

1. In a bowl, combine canned tuna, chopped celery, chopped red onion, chopped dill pickles, mayonnaise, Dijon mustard, lemon juice, salt, and pepper.
2. Mix until well combined and the tuna salad is evenly coated.
3. Place butter lettuce leaves on a serving platter.
4. Spoon tuna salad onto lettuce.
5. Top with halved cherry tomatoes and garnish with fresh dill.
6. Serve the tuna salad lettuce cups as a light and refreshing meal.

**Estimated time: 15 minutes**

**Nutritional information (per serving):**

- Calories: 180
- Protein: 20g
- Fat: 9g
- Carbohydrates: 4g

**Shopping list**: canned tuna, celery, red onion, dill pickles, mayonnaise, Dijon mustard, lemon, butter lettuce, cherry tomatoes, fresh dill

Tuna Salad Lettuce Cups

# Black Bean and Corn Quesadillas

## Ingredients:

- Black beans, rinsed and drained
- Corn kernels, fresh or frozen
- Red bell pepper, diced
- Red onion, diced
- Jalapeno, seeded and minced (optional)
- Cumin
- Chili powder
- Salt and pepper
- Whole wheat tortillas
- Shredded cheese (such as cheddar or Monterey Jack)
- Fresh cilantro, chopped
- Salsa and Greek yogurt (optional, for serving)

## Instructions:

1. In a large bowl, combine black beans, corn kernels, diced red bell pepper, diced red onion, minced jalapeno (if using), cumin, chili powder, salt, and pepper.
2. Heat a large skillet over medium heat and lightly coat with cooking spray or olive oil.
3. Place a whole wheat tortilla in the skillet and sprinkle with shredded cheese.
4. Spoon a generous amount of the black bean and corn mixture over half of the tortilla.
5. Fold the tortilla in half and press to seal.

6. Cook for 2-3 minutes per side until crispy and the cheese melt.
7. Repeat with the remaining tortillas and filling.
8. Cut the quesadillas into wedges and garnish with chopped cilantro.
9. Serve with salsa and Greek yogurt on the side, if desired.

**Estimated time: 20 minutes**

**Nutritional information (per serving):**

- Calories: 320
- Protein: 14g
- Fat: 9g
- Carbohydrates: 50g

**Shopping list:** black beans, corn kernels, red bell pepper, red onion, jalapeno (optional), cumin, chili powder, whole wheat tortillas, shredded cheese, fresh cilantro, salsa, Greek yogurt

Black Bean and Corn Quesadillas

# Asian Chicken Lettuce Wraps

## Ingredients:

- Ground chicken or turkey
- Garlic, minced
- Ginger, grated
- Soy sauce or tamari
- Hoisin sauce
- Rice vinegar
- Sesame oil
- Green onions, chopped
- Carrots, grated
- Water chestnuts, chopped
- Bibb or butter lettuce leaves
- Fresh cilantro, for garnish
- Lime wedges, for serving

## Instructions:

1. Heat skillet/wok over medium-high heat.
2. Add ground chicken or turkey and cook until browned and cooked through, breaking it up with a spoon as it cooks.
3. Add minced garlic and grated ginger to the skillet and cook for 1 minute.
4. In a small bowl, whisk together soy sauce or tamari, hoisin sauce, rice vinegar, and sesame oil.
5. Pour the sauce mixture into the skillet with the cooked chicken and stir to coat.

6. Add chopped green onions, grated carrots, and chopped water chestnuts to the skillet and cook for an additional 2-3 minutes, until the vegetables are tender.
7. Remove from heat and let cool slightly.
8. Spoon the chicken mixture onto individual lettuce leaves.
9. Garnish with the cilantro and serve with lime wedges.

**Estimated time: 25 minutes**

**Nutritional information** (per serving):

- Calories: 280
- Protein: 25g
- Fat: 12g
- Carbohydrates: 15g

**Shopping list:** ground chicken or turkey, garlic, ginger, soy sauce or tamari, hoisin sauce, rice vinegar, sesame oil, green onions, carrots, water chestnuts, bibb or butter lettuce, fresh cilantro, lime

Asian Chicken Lettuce Wraps

## Quinoa and Lentil Salad

**Ingredients:**

- Cooked quinoa
- Cooked lentils
- Cucumber, diced
- Cherry tomatoes, halved
- Red onion, thinly sliced
- Fresh parsley, chopped
- Lemon juice
- Olive oil
- Salt and pepper

**Instructions:**

1. In a large bowl, combine cooked quinoa, cooked lentils, diced cucumber, halved cherry tomatoes, thinly sliced red onion, and chopped fresh parsley.
2. Whisk lemon juice, olive oil, salt, and pepper in a small bowl for dressing.
3. Pour the dressing over the salad ingredients and toss to coat everything evenly.
4. Adjust the seasoning if needed.
5. Serve the quinoa and lentil salad chilled or at room temperature as a nutritious and filling lunch option.

**Estimated time: 15 minutes**

**Nutritional information (per serving):**

- Calories: 220
- Protein: 10g

- Fat: 4g
- Carbohydrates: 35g

**Shopping list**: cooked quinoa, cooked lentils, cucumber, cherry tomatoes, red onion, fresh parsley, lemon, olive oil

Quinoa and Lentil Salad

# Moroccan Spiced Chickpea Salad

**Ingredients:**

- Chickpeas, drained and rinsed
- Red bell pepper, diced
- Cucumber, diced
- Red onion, finely chopped
- Fresh cilantro, chopped
- Lemon juice
- Olive oil
- Ground cumin
- Ground coriander
- Ground paprika
- Ground cinnamon
- Salt and pepper
- Mixed greens, for serving

**Instructions:**

1. In a large bowl, combine chickpeas, diced red bell pepper, diced cucumber, finely chopped red onion, and chopped fresh cilantro.
2. In a small bowl, whisk together lemon juice, olive oil, ground cumin, ground coriander, ground paprika, ground cinnamon, salt, and pepper to make the dressing.
3. Pour the dressing over the salad ingredients and toss to coat everything evenly.
4. Refrigerate salad for at least 30 minutes to allow flavors to meld.

5. Serve the Moroccan spiced chickpea salad over a bed of mixed greens for a vibrant and satisfying meal.

**Estimated time: 20 minutes (plus marinating time)**

**Nutritional information (per serving):**

- Calories: 250
- Protein: 9g
- Fat: 8g
- Carbohydrates: 38g

**Shopping list**: chickpeas, red bell pepper, cucumber, red onion, fresh cilantro, lemon, olive oil, ground cumin, ground coriander, ground paprika, ground cinnamon, mixed greens

Moroccan Spiced Chickpea Salad

# CHAPTER 6

## DINNER RECIPES

### Baked Salmon with Lemon-Dill Sauce

**Ingredients:**

- Salmon fillets
- Lemon juice
- Fresh dill, chopped
- Garlic powder
- Salt and pepper

**Instructions:**

1. Preheat your oven to 400°F (200°C) and line the baking sheet with parchment paper.
2. Put salmon fillets on a baking sheet.
3. Drizzle lemon juice over the salmon and sprinkle with chopped dill, garlic powder, salt, and pepper.
4. Bake for 12-15 minutes until salmon is cooked and flakes easily.
5. Serve the baked salmon with a squeeze of fresh lemon juice and additional chopped dill on top.

**Estimated time: 20 minutes**

**Nutritional information** (per serving):

Calories: 250, Protein: 30g, Fat: 12g, Carbohydrates: 2g

**Shopping list:** salmon fillets, lemon, fresh dill, garlic powder

# Quinoa-Stuffed Zucchini Boats

**Ingredients:**

- Zucchini
- Cooked quinoa
- Onion, diced
- Bell pepper, diced
- Garlic, minced
- Tomato sauce
- Italian seasoning
- Mozzarella cheese, shredded (optional)
- Fresh basil, chopped (for garnish)

**Instructions:**

1. Preheat the oven to 375°F (190°C) and prepare a baking dish.
2. Cut the zucchini in half lengthwise and scoop out the flesh to create boat-shaped shells.
3. In a skillet, sauté the diced onion, bell pepper, and minced garlic until softened.
4. Add the cooked quinoa, tomato sauce, and Italian seasoning to the skillet and stir to combine.
5. Spoon the quinoa mixture into the zucchini boats and place them in the baking dish.
6. If desired, sprinkle shredded mozzarella cheese on top of the stuffed zucchini.
7. Bake for 20-25 minutes, or until the zucchini is tender and the filling is heated through.
8. Garnish with fresh basil before serving.

**Estimated time: 45 minutes**

**Nutritional information (per serving):**

- Calories: 180
- Protein: 8g
- Fat: 4g
- Carbohydrates: 30g

**Shopping list:** zucchini, cooked quinoa, onion, bell pepper, garlic, tomato sauce, Italian seasoning, mozzarella cheese (optional), fresh basil

Quinoa stutted zucchini boats

# Chicken Stir-Fry with Vegetables

**Ingredients:**

- Chicken breast, sliced
- Soy sauce (or tamari for gluten-free)
- Sesame oil
- Garlic, minced
- Ginger, grated
- Broccoli florets
- Bell peppers, sliced
- Carrots, julienned
- Snap peas
- Green onions, chopped (for garnish)
- Sesame seeds (for garnish)

**Instructions:**

1. In a bowl, marinate the sliced chicken breast in soy sauce and sesame oil for at least 15 minutes.
2. In a wok or large skillet, heat some sesame oil over medium-high heat.
3. Add the minced garlic and grated ginger to the hot oil and sauté until fragrant.
4. Add the marinated chicken to the wok and stir-fry until cooked through.
5. Add the broccoli florets, sliced bell peppers, julienned carrots, and snap peas to the wok and continue stir-frying for a few minutes until the vegetables are tender-crisp.
6. Season with additional soy sauce if desired.

7. Garnish the stir-fry with chopped green onions and sesame seeds before serving.

**Estimated time: 30 minutes**

**Nutritional information (per serving):**

- Calories: 250
- Protein: 25g
- Fat: 8g
- Carbohydrates: 20g

**Shopping list:** chicken breast, soy sauce, sesame oil, garlic, ginger, broccoli florets, bell peppers, carrots, snap peas, green onions, sesame seeds

Chicken stir fry with vegetables

# Roasted Vegetable and Chickpea Quinoa Bowl

## Ingredients:

- Cooked quinoa
- Chickpeas, drained and rinsed
- Mixed vegetables (such as bell peppers, zucchini, eggplant, and cherry tomatoes), chopped
- Red onion, sliced
- Olive oil
- Balsamic vinegar
- Dried herbs (such as oregano, thyme, and basil)
- Salt and pepper
- Fresh parsley, chopped (for garnish)

## Instructions:

1. Preheat your oven to 425°F (220°C) and line the baking sheet with parchment paper.
2. In a bowl, toss the mixed vegetables and sliced red onion with olive oil, balsamic vinegar, dried herbs, salt, and pepper.
3. Spread the vegetable mixture in a single layer on the prepared baking sheet.
4. Roast in the oven for 20-25 minutes, or until the vegetables are tender and slightly caramelized.
5. In a separate bowl, combine the cooked quinoa and drained/rinsed chickpeas.
6. Divide the quinoa and chickpea mixture into bowls and top with the roasted vegetables.

7. Garnish with fresh parsley before serving.

**Estimated time: 40 minutes**

**Nutritional information (per serving):**

- Calories: 280
- Protein: 10g
- Fat: 7g
- Carbohydrates: 45g

**Shopping list:** cooked quinoa, chickpeas, mixed vegetables (bell peppers, zucchini, eggplant, cherry tomatoes), red onion, olive oil, balsamic vinegar, dried herbs (oregano, thyme, basil), fresh parsley

# Lentil Curry with Brown Rice
## Ingredients:

- Brown rice
- Green lentils, cooked
- Onion, diced
- Garlic, minced
- Ginger, grated
- Curry powder
- Turmeric powder
- Cumin powder
- Crushed tomatoes
- Coconut milk
- Vegetable broth
- Spinach leaves
- Fresh cilantro, chopped (for garnish)

## Instructions:

1. Cook brown rice per package instructions, then set aside.
2. In a large pot or skillet, sauté the diced onion, minced garlic, and grated ginger until softened.
3. Add curry powder, turmeric powder, and cumin powder to the pot and cook for a minute to release the flavors.
4. Stir in crushed tomatoes, coconut milk, and vegetable broth, and bring to a simmer.

5. Add cooked lentils to the pot and let the curry simmer for 10-15 minutes to allow the flavors to meld together.
6. Just before serving, add spinach leaves and cook until wilted.
7. Serve the lentil curry over brown rice and garnish with chopped cilantro.

**Estimated time: 40 minutes**

**Nutritional information (per serving):**

- Calories: 320
- Protein: 14g
- Fat: 7g
- Carbohydrates: 52g

**Shopping list:** brown rice, green lentils, onion, garlic, ginger, curry powder, turmeric powder, cumin powder, crushed tomatoes, coconut milk, vegetable broth, spinach leaves, fresh cilantro

# Baked Turkey Meatballs with Zoodles

**Ingredients:**

- Ground turkey
- Breadcrumbs (gluten-free if needed)
- Egg
- Onion, finely chopped
- Garlic, minced
- Fresh parsley, chopped
- Salt and pepper
- Olive oil
- Zucchini, spiralized into zoodles
- Marinara sauce
- Grated Parmesan cheese (optional, omit for dairy-free)

**Instructions:**

1. Preheat your oven to 400°F (200°C) and line the baking sheet with parchment paper.
2. In a bowl, combine ground turkey, breadcrumbs, egg, finely chopped onion, minced garlic, chopped parsley, salt, and pepper. Mix until well combined.
3. Shape the mixture into meatballs and place them on the prepared baking sheet.
4. Drizzle the meatballs with olive oil and bake in the preheated oven for 20-25 minutes, or until cooked through and browned.
5. While the meatballs are baking, spiralize the zucchini into zoodles using a spiralizer.

6. Heat olive oil in a large skillet and set over medium heat. Add zoodles to skillet and sauté until tender, for a few minutes.
7. Serve the baked turkey meatballs over the zoodles and top with marinara sauce. Sprinkle with grated Parmesan cheese, if desired.

**Estimated time: 45 minutes**

**Nutritional information (per serving):**

- Calories: 320
- Protein: 25g
- Fat: 14g
- Carbohydrates: 25g

**Shopping list:** ground turkey, breadcrumbs (gluten-free if needed), egg, onion, garlic, fresh parsley, salt, pepper, olive oil, zucchini, marinara sauce, grated Parmesan cheese (optional)

# Teriyaki Tofu Stir-Fry

**Ingredients:**

- Firm tofu, cubed
- Teriyaki sauce (store-bought or homemade)
- Sesame oil
- Garlic, minced
- Ginger, grated
- Assorted stir-fry vegetables (such as bell peppers, broccoli, carrots, and snap peas), sliced or chopped
- Cooked rice or noodles of your choice

**Instructions:**

1. In a bowl, marinate the cubed tofu in teriyaki sauce for 15-20 minutes.
2. Heat sesame oil in a large skillet/wok over medium-high heat. Add minced garlic and grated ginger and sauté until fragrant.
3. Add the marinated tofu to the skillet and cook until golden brown on all sides.
4. Add the sliced or chopped stir-fry vegetables to the skillet and stir-fry until tender-crisp.
5. Pour in additional teriyaki sauce to coat the tofu and vegetables.
6. Serve the teriyaki tofu stir-fry over cooked rice or noodles.

**Estimated time: 30 minutes**

**Nutritional information (per serving):**

- Calories: 280
- Protein: 12g
- Fat: 10g
- Carbohydrates: 35g

**Shopping list:** firm tofu, teriyaki sauce, sesame oil, garlic, ginger, assorted stir-fried vegetables (bell peppers, broccoli, carrots, snap peas), cooked rice or noodles

# Stuffed Bell Peppers with Quinoa and Ground Beef

**Ingredients:**

- Bell peppers (any color), halved and seeds removed
- Ground beef
- Onion, finely chopped
- Garlic, minced
- Cooked quinoa
- Tomato sauce
- Italian seasoning
- Salt and pepper
- Shredded cheese (such as cheddar or mozzarella) for topping (optional, omit for dairy-free)

**Instructions:**

1. Preheat the oven to 375°F (190°C).
2. Cook ground beef in a skillet over medium heat until browned. Drain any excess fat.
3. Add the chopped onion and minced garlic to the skillet, and cook them until softened.
4. Stir in the cooked quinoa, tomato sauce, Italian seasoning, salt, and pepper. Cook them for a few minutes to combine flavors. Cook for a few more minutes to combine the flavors.
5. Spoon the beef and quinoa mixture into the halved bell peppers.

6. Put stuffed peppers in a baking dish, and cover with foil.
7. Bake in preheated oven for 25-30 minutes until bell peppers are tender.
8. Remove the foil, sprinkle the tops with shredded cheese (if using), and bake for an additional 5 minutes, or until the cheese is melted and bubbly.
9. Serve the stuffed bell peppers hot.

**Estimated time: 50 minutes**

**Nutritional information (per serving):**

- Calories: 320
- Protein: 22g
- Fat: 14g
- Carbohydrates: 25g

**Shopping list:** bell peppers, ground beef, onion, garlic, cooked quinoa, tomato sauce, Italian seasoning, salt, pepper, shredded cheese (optional)

# Grilled Shrimp Skewers with Citrus Marinade

**Ingredients:**

- Shrimp, peeled and deveined
- Olive oil
- Lemon juice
- Orange juice
- Garlic, minced
- Fresh parsley, chopped
- Salt and pepper
- Skewers (metal or soaked wooden skewers)

**Instructions:**

1. In a bowl, whisk together olive oil, lemon juice, orange juice, minced garlic, chopped parsley, salt, and pepper to make the citrus marinade.
2. Thread the shrimp onto skewers.
3. Place the shrimp skewers in a shallow dish and pour the citrus marinade over them. Refrigerate and let marinate for at least 30 minutes.
4. Preheat the grill to medium heat.
5. Grill the shrimp skewers for 2-3 minutes per side, or until the shrimp are opaque and cooked through.
6. Remove the shrimp skewers from the grill and serve hot.

**Estimated time: 40 minutes (including marinating time)**

**Nutritional information (per serving):**

- Calories: 180
- Protein: 25g
- Fat: 7g
- Carbohydrates: 2g

**Shopping list:** shrimp, olive oil, lemon juice, orange juice, garlic, fresh parsley, salt, pepper, skewers

# Sweet Potato and Black Bean Enchiladas

**Ingredients:**

- Sweet potatoes, peeled and diced
- Olive oil
- Onion, chopped
- Garlic, minced
- Canned black beans, drained and rinsed
- Cumin
- Chili powder
- Salt and pepper
- Corn tortillas
- Enchilada sauce (store-bought or homemade)
- Shredded cheese (such as cheddar or Mexican blend) for topping (optional, omit for dairy-free)

**Instructions:**

1. Preheat the oven to 375°F (190°C).
2. Put diced sweet potatoes on a baking sheet. Drizzle olive oil and sprinkle salt and pepper. Toss to coat.
3. Roast sweet potatoes in preheated oven for about 20-25 minutes until tender.
4. Heat olive oil in a skillet over medium heat. Put the sauté chopped onion and minced garlic until softened.
5. Stir in the black beans, roasted sweet potatoes, cumin, chili powder, salt, and pepper. Cook for a few minutes to blend in flavors together.

6. Warm the corn tortillas in a dry skillet or wrap them in a damp paper towel and microwave for a few seconds to make them pliable.
7. Spoon the sweet potato and black bean mixture onto each tortilla and roll them up. Put rolled enchiladas in a baking dish.
8. Pour enchilada sauce over the top of the rolled enchiladas, spreading it evenly.
9. If desired, sprinkle shredded cheese on top of the enchiladas.
10. Bake in the preheated oven for 15-20 minutes, or until the enchiladas are heated through and the cheese is melted and bubbly.
11. Serve hot sweet potato and black bean enchiladas.

**Estimated time: 1 hour**

**Nutritional information (per serving):**

- Calories: 320
- Protein: 11g
- Fat: 8g
- Carbohydrates: 54g

**Shopping list:** sweet potatoes, olive oil, onion, garlic, canned black beans, cumin, chili powder, salt, pepper, corn tortillas, enchilada sauce, shredded cheese (optional)

# Lemon Herb Roasted Chicken with Vegetables

## Ingredients:

- Chicken breasts or thighs
- Lemon, sliced
- Fresh herbs (such as thyme, rosemary, or parsley), chopped
- Olive oil
- Garlic, minced
- Salt and pepper
- Assorted vegetables (such as carrots, potatoes, and Brussels sprouts), chopped
- Optional: additional seasonings like paprika or dried herbs

## Instructions:

1. Preheat the oven to 425°F (220°C).
2. Place the chicken breasts or thighs in a baking dish. Place lemon slices on top of the chicken.
3. In a small bowl, mix the chopped fresh herbs, olive oil, minced garlic, salt, and pepper.
4. Rub the herb mixture all over the chicken, making sure to coat it evenly.
5. Add the chopped vegetables to the baking dish, arranging them around the chicken.
6. Optional: Sprinkle additional seasonings like paprika or dried herbs over the chicken and vegetables.

7. Place the baking dish in the preheated oven and roast for about 25-30 minutes, or until the chicken is cooked through and the vegetables are tender.
8. Remove from oven and let rest briefly before serving.

**Estimated time: 40 minutes**

**Nutritional information (per serving):**

- Calories: 300
- Protein: 30g
- Fat: 12g
- Carbohydrates: 15g

**Shopping list:** chicken breasts or thighs, lemon, fresh herbs (thyme, rosemary, or parsley), olive oil, garlic, salt, pepper, assorted vegetables (carrots, potatoes, Brussels sprouts), optional seasonings (paprika, dried herbs)

# Cauliflower Fried Rice with Tofu

**Ingredients:**

- Cauliflower, riced or grated
- Firm tofu, cubed
- Soy sauce or tamari
- Sesame oil
- Onion, chopped
- Garlic, minced
- Mixed vegetables (such as peas, carrots, and bell peppers), chopped
- Green onions, chopped (for garnish)
- Optional: beaten eggs (for non-vegan version)

**Instructions:**

1. Heat the sesame oil in a large skillet/wok over medium heat.
2. Add the cubed tofu to the skillet and cook until it becomes golden and slightly crispy. Take the tofu out of the skillet and set aside.
3. Add chopped onion and minced garlic to the same skillet. Sauté until the onion becomes translucent.
4. Add the mixed vegetables to the skillet and stir-fry until they are cooked but still slightly crisp.
5. Push the vegetables to one side of the skillet and add the riced cauliflower to the other side. Stir-fry the cauliflower for a few minutes until it becomes tender.
6. If using, push the cauliflower and vegetables to one side of the skillet and pour the beaten eggs into the

other side. Scramble the eggs until cooked, then mix them with the cauliflower and vegetables.

7. Add the cooked tofu back to the skillet and drizzle soy sauce or tamari over the mixture. Stir-fry for a few more minutes to combine the flavors.
8. Take off the heat and garnish with chopped green onions.
9. Serve the cauliflower fried rice with tofu hot.

**Estimated time: 30 minutes**

**Nutritional information (per serving):**

- Calories: 250
- Protein: 18g
- Fat: 12g
- Carbohydrates: 20g

**Shopping list:** cauliflower, firm tofu, soy sauce or tamari, sesame oil, onion, garlic, mixed vegetables (peas, carrots, bell peppers), green onions, optional eggs

Cauliflower Fried Rice with Tofu

# Eggplant Parmesan with Whole Wheat Pasta

**Ingredients:**

- Eggplant, sliced into rounds
- Whole wheat pasta
- Tomato sauce
- Mozzarella cheese, shredded
- Parmesan cheese, grated
- Breadcrumbs (use gluten-free breadcrumbs for a gluten-free version)
- Italian seasoning
- Garlic powder
- Salt and pepper
- Olive oil

**Instructions:**

1. Preheat the oven to 375°F (190°C).
2. Place the eggplant slices on a baking sheet and brush them with olive oil on both sides.
3. In a shallow dish, combine breadcrumbs, Italian seasoning, garlic powder, salt, and pepper.
4. Dip each eggplant slice into the breadcrumb mixture, coating both sides.
5. Arrange the breaded eggplant slices on the baking sheet and bake in the preheated oven for about 20 minutes, or until they are golden and crispy.
6. Meanwhile, cook the whole wheat pasta according to the package instructions.

7. In a saucepan, heat the tomato sauce over medium heat until warmed through.
8. Once the eggplant slices are cooked, remove them from the oven and set aside.
9. In a baking dish, layer tomato sauce, cooked pasta, and eggplant slices. Repeat layers until all ingredients are well used.
10. Top the dish with shredded mozzarella cheese and grated Parmesan cheese.
11. Bake in the oven for 15-20 minutes until cheese is melted and bubbly.
12. Remove from oven and set aside to cool briefly before serving.

**Estimated time: 1 hour**

**Nutritional information (per serving):**

- Calories: 400
- Protein: 20g
- Fat: 10g
- Carbohydrates: 60g

**Shopping list**: eggplant, whole wheat pasta, tomato sauce, mozzarella cheese, Parmesan cheese, breadcrumbs, Italian seasoning, garlic powder, salt, pepper, olive oil

# Thai Coconut Curry with Vegetables and Tofu

**Ingredients:**

- Firm tofu, cubed
- Assorted vegetables (such as bell peppers, broccoli, carrots, and snap peas), chopped
- Coconut milk
- Red curry paste
- Soy sauce or tamari
- Lime juice
- Brown sugar or coconut sugar
- Fresh cilantro, chopped (for garnish)
- Optional: Thai basil leaves (for garnish)

**Instructions:**

1. Heat a large skillet or wok over medium heat and add a drizzle of oil.
2. Add the cubed tofu to the skillet and cook until it becomes golden and slightly crispy. Take the tofu out of the skillet and set aside.
3. In the same skillet, add the chopped vegetables and stir-fry until they are cooked but still slightly crisp.
4. Push the vegetables to one side of the skillet and add the red curry paste to the other side. Stir-fry the curry paste for a minute to release its flavors.

5. Pour in the coconut milk, soy sauce or tamari, lime juice, and brown sugar or coconut sugar. Stir everything together until well combined.
6. Add the cooked tofu back to the skillet and stir to coat it with the curry sauce.
7. Continue to cook for a few more minutes until the tofu is heated through and the flavors are well blended.
8. Remove from heat and garnish with fresh cilantro and Thai basil leaves.
9. Serve the Thai coconut curry with vegetables and tofu over steamed rice or quinoa.

**Estimated time: 30 minutes**

**Nutritional information (per serving):**

- Calories: 300
- Protein: 15g
- Fat: 20g
- Carbohydrates: 20g

**Shopping list**: firm tofu, assorted vegetables (bell peppers, broccoli, carrots, snap peas), coconut milk, red curry paste, soy sauce or tamari, lime juice, brown sugar or coconut sugar, fresh cilantro, optional Thai basil leaves

# Quinoa-Stuffed Portobello Mushrooms

**Ingredients:**

- Portobello mushrooms
- Quinoa
- Vegetable broth or water
- Onion, diced
- Garlic, minced
- Spinach or kale, chopped
- Sun-dried tomatoes, chopped
- Feta cheese, crumbled (optional, omit for vegan version)
- Fresh parsley, chopped
- Olive oil
- Salt and pepper

**Instructions:**

1. Preheat the oven to 375°F (190°C).
2. Detach the stems from the portobello mushrooms and carefully scoop out the gills using a spoon.
3. Arrange the mushrooms on a baking sheet, ensuring the gill side faces upwards.
4. In a saucepan, combine quinoa and vegetable broth or water. Bring to a boil, then reduce heat and simmer for about 15 minutes, or until the quinoa is cooked and the liquid is absorbed.
5. Heat olive oil in a skillet over medium heat. Incorporate the diced onion and minced garlic

into the skillet and cook them until the onion turns translucent.

6. Add chopped spinach or kale to the skillet and cook until wilted.
7. Remove the skillet from heat and stir in the cooked quinoa, chopped sun-dried tomatoes, crumbled feta cheese (if using), and fresh parsley. Season with salt and pepper to taste.
8. Spoon the quinoa mixture into the portobello mushrooms, filling them generously.
9. Place the baking sheet with the stuffed mushrooms in the preheated oven and bake for about 20 minutes, or until the mushrooms are tender and the filling is heated through.
10. Take it out of the oven and allow it to cool for a few minutes before serving.

**Estimated time: 45 minutes**

**Nutritional information (per serving):**

- Calories: 250
- Protein: 12g
- Fat: 8g
- Carbohydrates: 35g

**Shopping list:** portobello mushrooms, quinoa, vegetable broth or water, onion, garlic, spinach or kale, sun-dried tomatoes, feta cheese (optional), fresh parsley, olive oil, salt, pepper

Apple Cinnamon Quinoa Breakfast Cookies

Zucchini and Salmon Cakes

# CHAPTER 7

## DESSERT RECIPES

### Chocolate Avocado Mousse

**Ingredients:**

- Ripe avocados
- Cocoa powder
- Maple syrup or honey
- Vanilla extract
- Almond milk or any other non-dairy milk
- Optional toppings: fresh berries, chopped nuts

**Instructions:**

1. In a blender or food processor, combine avocados, cocoa powder, maple syrup or honey, vanilla extract, and almond milk.
2. Blend until smooth and creamy.
3. Transfer the mousse to serving dishes and refrigerate for at least 1 hour to set.
4. Serve chilled, topped with fresh berries or chopped nuts if desired.

**Estimated time: 10 minutes**

**Nutritional information** (per serving): Calories: 150 - Protein: 3g - Fat: 12g- Carbohydrates: 10g

**Shopping list:** ripe avocados, cocoa powder, maple syrup or honey, vanilla extract, almond milk, optional fresh berries, optional chopped nuts

# Berry Crumble Bars

**Ingredients:**

- Rolled oats
- Almond flour
- Coconut oil
- Maple syrup or honey
- Mixed berries (such as strawberries, blueberries, and raspberries)
- Lemon juice
- Cornstarch or arrowroot powder
- Optional: sliced almonds or shredded coconut (for topping)

**Instructions:**

1. Preheat the oven to 350°F (175°C) and line a baking dish with parchment paper.
2. In a mixing bowl, combine rolled oats, almond flour, melted coconut oil, and maple syrup or honey. Mix until the ingredients are well combined and crumbly.
3. Set aside ½ cup of the oat mixture for the topping and press the remaining mixture into the prepared baking dish to form the crust.
4. In a separate bowl, toss the mixed berries with lemon juice, cornstarch or arrowroot powder, and a sweetener of your choice (if desired).
5. Spread the berry mixture evenly over the crust in the baking dish.

6. Sprinkle the reserved oat mixture on top of the berries.
7. Optional: Sprinkle sliced almonds or shredded coconut over the crumble topping.
8. Bake in the preheated oven for about 30-35 minutes, or until the top is golden brown and the berries are bubbling.
9. Take it out of the oven and let it cool down completely before cutting it into bars.

**Estimated time: 1 hour**

**Nutritional information (per serving):**

- Calories: 180
- Protein: 3g
- Fat: 8g
- Carbohydrates: 25g

**Shopping list:** rolled oats, almond flour, coconut oil, maple syrup or honey, mixed berries, lemon juice, cornstarch or arrowroot powder, optional sliced almonds or shredded coconut

# Banana Nut Bread

**Ingredients:**

- Ripe bananas
- Almond flour
- Coconut flour
- Eggs
- Maple syrup or honey
- Coconut oil, melted
- Baking powder
- Cinnamon
- Chopped walnuts or pecans (optional)

**Instructions:**

1. Preheat the oven to 350°F (175°C) and grease a loaf pan.
2. In a mixing bowl, thoroughly mash the ripe bananas until they achieve a smooth consistency.
3. Add almond flour, coconut flour, eggs, maple syrup or honey, melted coconut oil, baking powder, and cinnamon to the bowl. Thoroughly combine all the ingredients, ensuring they are well mixed together.
4. If desired, gently incorporate chopped walnuts or pecans into the mixture by folding them in.
5. Pour the batter into the loaf pan that has been prepared, ensuring it is spread evenly across the pan.

6. Bake in the preheated oven for about 45-50 minutes, or until a toothpick inserted into the center comes out clean.
7. Remove from the oven and let it cool in the pan for a few minutes before transferring to a wire rack to cool completely.

**Estimated time: 1 hour**

**Nutritional information (per serving):**

- Calories: 200
- Protein: 6g
- Fat: 12g
- Carbohydrates: 20g

**Shopping list**: ripe bananas, almond flour, coconut flour, eggs, maple syrup or honey, coconut oil, baking powder, cinnamon, optional chopped walnuts or pecans

Banana Nut Bread

# Coconut Chia Seed Pudding

**Ingredients:**

- Coconut milk
- Chia seeds
- Maple syrup or honey
- Vanilla extract
- Optional toppings: fresh berries, sliced almonds, shredded coconut

**Instructions:**

1. In a jar or bowl, combine coconut milk, chia seeds, maple syrup or honey, and vanilla extract. Stir well to combine all the ingredients.
2. Let the mixture sit for a few minutes, then stir again to prevent clumping of chia seeds.
3. Cover the jar or bowl and refrigerate overnight or for at least 4 hours to allow the chia seeds to absorb the liquid and form a pudding-like consistency.
4. After the pudding has fully set, give it a final stir to ensure all the ingredients are well incorporated.
5. Serve the coconut chia seed pudding chilled, topped with fresh berries, sliced almonds, shredded coconut, or any other desired toppings.

**Estimated time: 10 minutes (+ chilling time)**

**Nutritional information (per serving):**

Calories: 180, Protein: 5g, Fat: 12g, Carbohydrates: 15g

**Shopping list:** coconut milk, chia seeds, maple syrup or honey, vanilla extract, optional fresh berries, optional sliced almonds, optional shredded coconut

Coconut Chia Seed Pudding

# Baked Apples with Cinnamon and Almonds

- Ingredients:
- Apples
- Cinnamon
- Chopped almonds
- Maple syrup or honey
- Optional: raisins, dried cranberries, or other dried fruits

## Instructions:

1. Preheat the oven to 375°F (190°C).
2. Core the apples using an apple corer or a knife, leaving the bottom intact.
3. Arrange the cored apples in a baking dish.
4. In a small bowl, combine cinnamon, chopped almonds, and maple syrup or honey. Optionally, add raisins, dried cranberries, or other dried fruits to the mixture.
5. Stuff the apple cavities with the cinnamon-almond mixture, pressing it down gently.
6. Drizzle a little extra maple syrup or honey over the top of each apple.
7. Bake in the preheated oven for about 25-30 minutes, or until the apples are tender.
8. Take them out of the oven and allow them to cool for a few minutes before serving.

## Estimated time: 40 minutes

**Nutritional information (per serving):**

- Calories: 150

- Protein: 3g

- Fat: 8g

- Carbohydrates: 20g

**Shopping list:** apples, cinnamon, chopped almonds, maple syrup or honey, optional raisins or dried cranberries

Baked Apples with Cinnamon and Almonds

## Mango Coconut Sorbet

**Ingredients:**

- Ripe mangoes
- Coconut milk
- Lime juice
- Sweetener of choice (optional)

**Instructions:**

1. Peel the ripe mangoes and cut them into small dice, removing the pit.
2. Transfer the diced mangoes into a blender or food processor.
3. Add coconut milk and lime juice to the blender.
4. Blend until smooth and creamy.
5. Taste the mixture and add a sweetener of your choice, such as honey or maple syrup, if desired. Blend again to incorporate the sweetener.
6. Carefully pour the mixture into a container that is safe for freezing, ensuring to cover it with a lid.
7. Put the container in the freezer and allow it to freeze for a minimum of 4 hours, or until it becomes firm.
8. Once frozen, remove the sorbet from the freezer and let it sit at room temperature for a few minutes to soften before serving.
9. Scoop the mango coconut sorbet into bowls or cones and enjoy!

**Estimated time: 10 minutes (+ freezing time)**

**Nutritional information (per serving):**

- Calories: 120

- Protein: 1g

- Fat: 5g

- Carbohydrates: 20g

**Shopping list:** ripe mangoes, coconut milk, lime juice, sweetener of choice (optional)

Mango Coconut Sorbet

# Peanut Butter Energy Balls

**Ingredients:**

- Rolled oats
- Peanut butter
- Honey or maple syrup
- Flaxseeds
- Chia seeds
- Mini chocolate chips (optional)
- Shredded coconut (optional)

**Instructions:**

1. In a mixing bowl, combine rolled oats, peanut butter, honey or maple syrup, flaxseeds, chia seeds, and mini chocolate chips (if using). Stir well to combine all the ingredients.
2. If the mixture seems too dry, add a little more peanut butter or honey/maple syrup. If it's too sticky, add more oats.
3. Once the mixture is well combined and holds together, use your hands to shape it into small bite-sized balls.
4. Optional: Roll the energy balls in shredded coconut for an extra touch of flavor and texture.
5. Place the energy balls on a baking sheet or plate lined with parchment paper.
6. Place the energy balls in the refrigerator and let them refrigerate for at least 30 minutes to allow them to firm up.

7. Once chilled, transfer the energy balls to an airtight container and store them in the refrigerator for up to a week.
8. Enjoy the peanut butter energy balls as a quick and nutritious snack on the go!

**Estimated time: 20 minutes (+ chilling time)**

**Nutritional information (per serving, about 2 balls):**

- Calories: 150

- Protein: 4g

- Fat: 8g

- Carbohydrates: 16g

**Shopping list**: rolled oats, peanut butter, honey or maple syrup, flaxseeds, chia seeds, mini chocolate chips (optional), shredded coconut (optional)

Peanut Butter Energy Balls

# Greek Yogurt Parfait with Fresh Fruit

**Ingredients:**

- Greek yogurt
- Fresh mixed berries (e.g., strawberries, blueberries, raspberries)
- Granola
- Honey (optional)

**Instructions:**

1. In a glass or bowl, layer Greek yogurt, fresh mixed berries, and granola.
2. Repeat the layers until you reach the desired amount of each ingredient.
3. If desired, drizzle honey on top of the energy balls to add a touch of sweetness.
4. Serve the Greek yogurt parfait immediately and enjoy!

**Estimated time: 5 minutes**

**Nutritional information (per serving):**

- Calories: 200
- Protein: 18g
- Fat: 3g
- Carbohydrates: 26g

**Shopping list:** Greek yogurt, fresh mixed berries, granola, honey (optional)

# Chocolate Peanut Butter Protein Smoothie

## Ingredients:

- Chocolate protein powder
- Peanut butter
- Banana
- Almond milk or any other milk of choice
- Ice cubes

## Instructions:

1. In a blender, combine chocolate protein powder, peanut butter, a ripe banana, almond milk, and a handful of ice cubes.
2. Blend until smooth and creamy.
3. If the smoothie has a thick consistency, you can add more almond milk to achieve the desired thickness. If the smoothie is too thin in consistency, you can add more ice cubes to thicken it up.
4. Pour the chocolate peanut butter protein smoothie into a glass or portable bottle.
5. Enjoy the smoothie immediately or refrigerate for later.

**Estimated time: 5 minutes**

**Nutritional information (per serving):**

Calories: 350- Protein: 25g Fat: 12g - Carbohydrates: 35g

**Shopping list**: chocolate protein powder, peanut butter, banana, almond milk or any other milk of choice, ice cubes

# Lemon Poppy Seed Muffins

**Ingredients:**

- Almond flour
- Lemon zest
- Poppy seeds
- Baking soda
- Salt
- Eggs
- Honey or maple syrup
- Lemon juice
- Coconut oil

**Instructions:**

1. Preheat the oven to 350°F (175°C) and line a muffin tin with paper liners.
2. In a mixing bowl, combine almond flour, lemon zest, poppy seeds, baking soda, and salt. Mix well.
3. In a separate bowl, whisk together eggs, honey or maple syrup, lemon juice, and melted coconut oil.
4. Combine the wet ingredients with the dry ingredients, stirring until they are thoroughly combined.
5. Distribute the batter evenly among the muffin cups, filling each one approximately two-thirds full.
6. Place the muffin tin in the oven and bake for 15-18 minutes, or until a toothpick inserted into the center of a muffin comes out clean.

7. Take the muffins out of the oven and allow them to cool in the tin for a few minutes before transferring them to a wire rack to cool completely.
8. Enjoy the lemon poppy seed muffins as a delicious and nutritious treat!

**Estimated time: 25 minutes**

**Nutritional information (per serving, 1 muffin):**

- Calories: 200
- Protein: 6g
- Fat: 15g
- Carbohydrates: 10g

**Shopping list**: almond flour, lemon zest, poppy seeds, baking soda, salt, eggs, honey or maple syrup, lemon juice, coconut oil

# Almond Flour Blueberry Muffins

## Ingredients:

- Almond flour
- Baking powder
- Salt
- Eggs
- Honey or maple syrup
- Almond milk
- Vanilla extract
- Fresh or frozen blueberries

## Instructions:

1. Preheat the oven to 350°F (175°C) and line a muffin tin with paper liners.
2. In a mixing bowl, whisk together almond flour, baking powder, and salt.
3. In a separate bowl, beat the eggs. Add honey or maple syrup, almond milk, and vanilla extract. Mix well.
4. Carefully pour the wet ingredients into the bowl containing the dry ingredients. Stir the mixture gently until the ingredients are just combined, being careful not to overmix.
5. Gently fold in the blueberries.
6. Distribute the batter evenly among the muffin cups, filling each one approximately two-thirds full.

7. Place the muffin tin in the oven and bake for 20-25 minutes, or until a toothpick inserted into the center of a muffin comes out clean.
8. Once baked, let the muffins cool in the tin for a few minutes before carefully transferring them to a wire rack to cool completely.
9. Enjoy the almond flour blueberry muffins as a delightful and wholesome treat!

**Estimated time: 30 minutes**

**Nutritional information (per serving, 1 muffin):**

- Calories: 150
- Protein: 5g
- Fat: 10g
- Carbohydrates: 12g

**Shopping list:** almond flour, baking powder, salt, eggs, honey or maple syrup, almond milk, vanilla extract, fresh or frozen blueberries

## Pumpkin Spice Energy Bites

Ingredients:

- Rolled oats
- Pumpkin puree
- Almond butter
- Honey or maple syrup
- Pumpkin spice
- Chia seeds
- Shredded coconut (optional)

Instructions:

1. In a mixing bowl, combine rolled oats, pumpkin puree, almond butter, honey or maple syrup, pumpkin spice, chia seeds, and shredded coconut (if using). Stir well to combine all the ingredients.
2. If the mixture seems too dry, add a little more almond butter or honey/maple syrup. If it's too sticky, add more oats.
3. Once the mixture is well combined, use your hands to shape it into small bite-sized balls.
4. Optional: Roll the energy bites in shredded coconut for additional flavor and texture.
5. Place the energy bites on a baking sheet or plate lined with parchment paper.
6. Refrigerate the energy bites for at least 30 minutes to allow them to firm up.

7. Once chilled, transfer the energy bites to an airtight container and store them in the refrigerator for up to a week.
8. Enjoy the pumpkin spice energy bites as a healthy and convenient snack!

**Estimated time: 20 minutes (+ chilling time)**

**Nutritional information (per serving, about 2 bites):**

- Calories: 150
- Protein: 4g
- Fat: 8g
- Carbohydrates: 16g

**Shopping list:** rolled oats, pumpkin puree, almond butter, honey or maple syrup, pumpkin spice, chia seeds, shredded coconut (optional)

Pumpkin Spice Energy Bites

# Mixed Berry Cobbler

**Ingredients:**

- Mixed berries (e.g., strawberries, blueberries, raspberries, blackberries)
- Lemon juice
- Honey or maple syrup
- Almond flour
- Rolled oats
- Almond butter
- Cinnamon
- Salt
- Coconut oil

**Instructions:**

1. Preheat the oven to 350°F (175°C).
2. In a mixing bowl, toss the mixed berries with lemon juice and honey or maple syrup.
3. Transfer the berry mixture to a baking dish.
4. In a separate bowl, combine almond flour, rolled oats, almond butter, cinnamon, salt, and coconut oil. Mix until the mixture resembles coarse crumbs.
5. Evenly sprinkle the crumble topping over the berries, ensuring they are well-covered.
6. Bake for 25-30 minutes or until the berries are bubbling and the topping is golden brown.
7. Take the cobbler out of the oven and allow it to cool for a few minutes before serving.

8. Serve the mixed berry cobbler warm with a scoop of your favorite dairy-free ice cream or whipped coconut cream, if desired.

9. Enjoy the mixed berry cobbler as a comforting and fruity dessert!

**Estimated time: 40 minutes**

**Nutritional information (per serving):**

- Calories: 200
- Protein: 4g
- Fat: 12g
- Carbohydrates: 20g

**Shopping list:** mixed berries (e.g., strawberries, blueberries, raspberries, blackberries), lemon juice, honey or maple syrup, almond flour, rolled oats, almond butter, cinnamon, salt, coconut oil

Mixed Berry Cobbler

# Vanilla Chia Pudding with Fresh Berries

- **Ingredients:**
- Chia seeds
- Almond milk or any other milk of choice
- Vanilla extract
- Honey or maple syrup
- Fresh berries (e.g., strawberries, blueberries, raspberries)

## Instructions:

1. In a bowl, combine chia seeds, almond milk, vanilla extract, and honey or maple syrup. Stir well to mix all the ingredients.
2. Allow the mixture to sit for 5 minutes, giving the chia seeds enough time to absorb the liquid. Stir again to prevent clumping.
3. Cover the bowl and refrigerate the chia pudding for at least 2 hours or overnight to thicken.
4. Once the chia pudding has thickened to your desired consistency, give it a good stir to break up any clumps.
5. Spoon the chia pudding into serving bowls or glasses.
6. Top the pudding with fresh berries.
7. Serve the vanilla chia pudding with fresh berries chilled and enjoy!

**Estimated time: 10 minutes (+ chilling time)**

## Nutritional information (per serving):

- Calories: 150
- Protein: 5g
- Fat: 8g
- Carbohydrates: 15g

**Shopping list:** chia seeds, almond milk or any other milk of choice, vanilla extract, honey or maple syrup, fresh berries (e.g., strawberries, blueberries, raspberries)

Vanilla Chia Pudding with Fresh Berries

# Apple Cinnamon Quinoa Breakfast Cookies

**Ingredients:**

- Quinoa flakes
- Almond flour
- Cinnamon
- Baking powder
- Salt
- Unsweetened applesauce
- Maple syrup
- Coconut oil
- Diced apple
- Chopped nuts (e.g., walnuts, pecans)
- Raisins or dried cranberries

**Instructions:**

1. To begin, preheat your oven to 350°F (175°C) and line a baking sheet with parchment paper.
2. In a mixing bowl, combine quinoa flakes, almond flour, cinnamon, baking powder, and salt.
3. In a separate bowl, mix unsweetened applesauce, maple syrup, and melted coconut oil.
4. Combine the wet ingredients with the dry ingredients and stir them together until they are thoroughly combined.
5. Fold in diced apples, chopped nuts, and raisins or dried cranberries.

6. Drop spoonfuls of the cookie dough onto the prepared baking sheet and flatten them slightly with the back of a spoon.
7. Place the baking sheet in the oven and bake for 15-18 minutes, or until the edges of the cookies turn golden brown.
8. Once baked, let the cookies cool on the baking sheet for a few minutes, then carefully transfer them to a wire rack to cool completely.
9. Enjoy the apple cinnamon quinoa breakfast cookies as a nutritious and portable breakfast or snack!

**Estimated time: 30 minutes**

**Nutritional information (per serving, 1 cookie):**

- Calories: 120
- Protein: 3g
- Fat: 6g
- Carbohydrates: 15g

**Shopping list:** quinoa flakes, almond flour, cinnamon, baking powder, salt, unsweetened applesauce, maple syrup, coconut oil, diced apple, chopped nuts (e.g., walnuts, pecans), raisins or dried cranberries

Tuna Poke Bowl

# CHAPTER 8

# GLUTEN-FREE RECIPES

## Quinoa Salad with Roasted Vegetables

**Ingredients:**

- 1 cup quinoa
- 2 cups vegetable broth or water
- Assorted vegetables for roasting (such as bell peppers, zucchini, eggplant, and cherry tomatoes)
- 2 tablespoons olive oil
- Salt and pepper to taste
- Fresh herbs for garnish (such as parsley or basil)

**Estimated Time: 40 minutes**

**Nutritional Information (per serving):**

- Calories: 250
- Protein: 8g
- Fat: 8g
- Carbohydrates: 37g

**Instructions:**

1. Rinse the quinoa under cold water, then combine it with vegetable broth or water in a saucepan.
2. Bring to a boil, then reduce the heat to low, cover, and simmer for about 15-20 minutes until the quinoa is cooked and the liquid is absorbed.

3. Preheat the oven to 425°F (220°C).
4. Cut the assorted vegetables into bite-sized pieces and place them on a baking sheet. Drizzle it with olive oil and season with salt and pepper.
5. Roast the vegetables in the preheated oven for 20-25 minutes, until they are tender and slightly charred.
6. Combine the cooked quinoa and the roasted vegetable in a large bowl, Toss gently to mix well.
7. Season with salt and pepper to taste.
8. Garnish with fresh herbs before serving.

**Shopping List:**

- Quinoa - Vegetable broth or water
- Assorted vegetables for roasting (such as bell peppers, zucchini, eggplant, and cherry tomatoes)
- Olive oil - Salt - Pepper
- Fresh herbs (such as parsley or basil)

# Cauliflower Pizza Crust

## Ingredients:

- 1 head cauliflower
- 2 eggs, lightly beaten
- 1/2 cup grated Parmesan cheese (or nutritional yeast for a vegan option)
- 1 teaspoon dried oregano
- 1/2 teaspoon garlic powder
- Salt and pepper to taste
- Pizza toppings of your choice

**Estimated Time: 45 minutes**

**Nutritional Information (per serving):**

- Calories: 180
- Protein: 13g
- Fat: 7g
- Carbohydrates: 19g

## Instructions:

1. Preheat the oven to 400°F (200°C). Line a baking sheet with parchment paper.
2. Cut the cauliflower into florets and pulse them in a food processor until they resemble rice.
3. Place the cauliflower rice in a microwave-safe bowl and microwave on high for 5-6 minutes, or until it becomes tender.
4. Allow the cooked cauliflower rice to cool for a few minutes, then transfer it to a clean kitchen towel or

cheesecloth. Squeeze out as much moisture as possible.

5. In a large bowl, combine the squeezed cauliflower rice, beaten eggs, grated Parmesan cheese (or nutritional yeast), dried oregano, garlic powder, salt, and pepper. Mix well until a dough-like consistency.

6. Transfer the cauliflower dough onto the prepared baking sheet and shape it into a pizza crust of your desired thickness.

7. Bake the crust in the preheated oven for 25-30 minutes, or until golden brown and firm.

8. Take the crust out of the oven and proceed to add your preferred pizza toppings.

9. Return the pizza to the oven and bake for an additional 10-15 minutes, or until the toppings are heated through. Slice and serve.

**Shopping List:**- 1 head cauliflower - Eggs

- Grated Parmesan cheese (or nutritional yeast)

- Dried oregano - Garlic powder - Salt

- Pepper - Pizza toppings of your choice

## Zucchini Noodles with Pesto

**Ingredients:**

- 2-3 medium zucchini
- 1 cup fresh basil leaves
- 1/4 cup pine nuts
- 1/4 cup grated Parmesan cheese (or nutritional yeast for a vegan option)
- 1 clove garlic
- 1/4 cup olive oil
- Salt and pepper to taste
- Cherry tomatoes for garnish (optional)

**Estimated Time: 20 minutes**

**Nutritional Information (per serving):**

- Calories: 200
- Protein: 7g
- Fat: 18g
- Carbohydrates: 7g

**Instructions:**

1. Using a spiralizer or a vegetable peeler, create zucchini noodles by cutting the zucchini into thin, noodle-like strips. Set aside.
2. In a food processor or blender, combine the fresh basil leaves, pine nuts, grated Parmesan cheese (or nutritional yeast), garlic, olive oil, salt, and pepper. Blend until smooth.

3. Heat a large skillet over medium heat. Add the zucchini noodles to the skillet and sauté for 2-3 minutes until they are slightly softened.
4. Remove the skillet from the heat and add the pesto sauce. Toss the noodles gently to coat them with the sauce.
5. Serve the zucchini noodles with cherry tomatoes as a garnish, if desired.

## Shopping List:

- Zucchini

- Fresh basil leaves

- Pine nuts

- Grated Parmesan cheese (or nutritional yeast)

- Garlic clove - Olive oil – Salt - Pepper

- Cherry tomatoes (optional)

# Baked Lemon Herb Chicken with Quinoa

## Ingredients:

- 4 boneless, skinless chicken breasts
- Juice of 1 lemon
- Zest of 1 lemon
- 2 tablespoons olive oil
- 2 cloves garlic, minced
- 1 teaspoon dried thyme
- 1 teaspoon dried rosemary
- Salt and pepper to taste
- 1 cup quinoa
- 2 cups vegetable broth or water
- Fresh parsley for garnish

**Estimated Time: 40 minutes**

## Nutritional Information (per serving):

- Calories: 350
- Protein: 30g
- Fat: 10g
- Carbohydrates: 30g

## Instructions:

1. Preheat the oven to 400°F (200°C). Lightly grease a baking dish.
2. In a small bowl, whisk together the lemon juice, lemon zest, olive oil, minced garlic, dried thyme, dried rosemary, salt, and pepper.
3. Place the chicken breasts in the prepared baking dish and pour the lemon herb marinade over them.

Make sure the chicken is evenly coated. Let it marinate for 15-20 minutes.

4. While the chicken is marinating, rinse the quinoa under cold water, then combine it with the vegetable broth or water in a saucepan. Bring to a boil, then reduce the heat to low, cover, and simmer for about 15-20 minutes until the quinoa is cooked and the liquid is absorbed.

5. After marinating, place the chicken breasts in the preheated oven and bake for 20-25 minutes, or until the chicken is cooked through and no longer pink in the center.

6. Take the chicken out of the oven and allow it to rest for a few minutes before serving.

7. Serve the baked lemon herb chicken over a bed of cooked quinoa.

8. Garnish with fresh parsley before serving.

## Shopping List:

- Boneless, skinless chicken breasts
- Lemons
- Olive oil
- Garlic cloves
- Dried thyme
- Dried rosemary
- Salt
- Pepper - Quinoa
- Vegetable broth or water - Fresh parsley

# Mexican Stuffed Bell Peppers with Brown Rice

**Ingredients:**

- 4 bell peppers (any color)
- 1 cup cooked brown rice
- 1 cup black beans, drained and rinsed
- 1 cup corn kernels
- 1 cup diced tomatoes
- 1/2 cup diced onion
- 1/2 cup diced bell pepper (from the tops of the stuffed peppers)
- 1 clove garlic, minced
- 1 teaspoon chili powder
- 1/2 teaspoon cumin
- Salt and pepper to taste
- Shredded dairy-free cheese for topping (optional)
- Fresh cilantro for garnish (optional)

**Estimated Time: 1 hour**

**Nutritional Information (per serving):**

- Calories: 300- Protein: 10g - Fat: 2g - Carbohydrates: 65g

**Instructions:**

1. Preheat the oven to 375°F (190°C). Cut off pepper tops and remove seeds/membranes. Set aside the tops for later use.
2. In a large bowl, combine the cooked brown rice, black beans, corn kernels, diced tomatoes, diced onion,

diced bell pepper (from the tops), minced garlic, chili powder, cumin, salt, and pepper. Mix well to combine.

3. Stuff each bell pepper with the rice and bean mixture, pressing it down gently to fill the peppers.
4. Position the stuffed peppers in an upright manner within a baking dish. If the peppers won't stand on their own, you can use foil to prop them up.
5. Cover the baking dish with foil and bake in the preheated oven for 40-45 minutes, or until the peppers are tender.
6. Remove the foil and sprinkle shredded dairy-free cheese on top of each stuffed pepper, if desired. Return the peppers to the oven and bake for an additional 5 minutes, or until the cheese is melted.
7. Take the peppers out of the oven and allow them to cool for a few minutes before serving.
8. Garnish with fresh cilantro, if desired.

**Shopping List:**

- Bell peppers (any color)
- Cooked brown rice
- Black beans - Corn kernels
- Diced tomatoes, Onion, Garlic clove, Chili powder
- Cumin, Salt, Pepper
- Shredded dairy-free cheese (optional)
- Fresh cilantro (optional)

# Gluten-Free Banana Bread

## - Ingredients:

- Ripe bananas
- Gluten-free flour blend
- Baking powder
- Baking soda
- Salt
- Ground cinnamon
- Eggs
- Coconut oil or melted butter
- Honey or maple syrup
- Vanilla extract
- Chopped nuts (optional)

## - Instructions:

1. Preheat the oven to 350°F (175°C) and grease a loaf pan with cooking spray or line it with parchment paper.
2. In a spacious bowl, use a fork to mash the ripe bananas until they achieve a smooth consistency.
3. Add gluten-free flour blend, baking powder, baking soda, salt, and ground cinnamon to the bowl. Stir until well combined.
4. In a separate bowl, whisk together eggs, coconut oil or melted butter, honey or maple syrup, and vanilla extract.
5. Pour the wet ingredients into the banana mixture and stir until everything is thoroughly combined.

6. If desired, fold in chopped nuts.
7. Transfer the batter into the loaf pan that has been prepared, and use a spatula to even out the top surface.
8. Place the loaf pan in the oven and bake for approximately 50-60 minutes, or until a toothpick inserted into the center of the bread comes out clean.
9. Remove the banana bread from the oven and let it cool in the pan for 10 minutes, then transfer it to a wire rack to cool completely.
10. Slice and enjoy the delicious gluten-free banana bread as a tasty snack or breakfast option!

   **- Estimated time: 1 hour 15 minutes**

   **- Nutritional information (per serving, 1 slice):**

- Calories: 180
- Protein: 3g
- - Fat: 8g    - Carbohydrates: 25g

**Shopping list**: ripe bananas, gluten-free flour blend, baking powder, baking soda, salt, ground cinnamon, eggs, coconut oil or melted butter, honey or maple syrup, vanilla extract, chopped nuts (optional)

# Mediterranean Chickpea Salad

## Ingredients:

- Chickpeas
- Cucumber
- Cherry tomatoes
- Red onion
- Kalamata olives
- Feta cheese
- Fresh parsley
- Lemon juice
- Extra virgin olive oil
- Garlic clove (optional)
- Salt and pepper to taste

- **Instructions:**

1. Rinse and drain the chickpeas, then transfer them to a large mixing bowl.
2. Chop the cucumber, cherry tomatoes, red onion, and kalamata olives into bite-sized pieces and add them to the bowl.
3. Crumble feta cheese over the salad.
4. Take fresh parsley and finely chop it before adding it to the bowl.
5. In a small bowl, whisk together lemon juice, extra virgin olive oil, minced garlic (optional), salt, and pepper.
6. Drizzle the dressing evenly over the salad and toss gently to ensure all the ingredients are coated.

7. Adjust the seasoning if needed.
8. Let the Mediterranean chickpea salad sit for at least 10 minutes to allow the flavors to meld together.
9. Serve the salad as a refreshing and protein-packed side dish or light lunch.

- **Estimated time: 15 minutes**

- **Nutritional information (per serving):**

- Calories: 220
- Protein: 8g
- Fat: 10g
- Carbohydrates: 25g

**Shopping list:**

chickpeas, cucumber, cherry tomatoes, red onion, kalamata olives, feta cheese, fresh parsley, lemon juice, extra virgin olive oil, garlic clove (optional), salt, pepper

# Shrimp Stir-Fry with Rice Noodles

## Ingredients:

- Rice noodles
- Shrimp
- Mixed vegetables (e.g., bell peppers, broccoli, carrots, snap peas)
- Garlic cloves
- Ginger
- Soy sauce (gluten-free if needed)
- Sesame oil
- Lime juice
- Red pepper flakes (optional)
- Salt and pepper to taste

## - Instructions:

1. Cook rice noodles as per package instructions. Drain and set aside.
2. Heat sesame oil in a large skillet or wok over medium-high heat.
3. Add minced garlic and grated ginger to the pan and sauté for about 1 minute until fragrant.
4. Add the mixed vegetables to the pan and stir-fry for 3-4 minutes until they start to soften.
5. Push the vegetables to one side of the pan and add the shrimp. Cook the shrimp for approximately 2-3 minutes on each side until they become pink and opaque in appearance.

6. In a small bowl, whisk together soy sauce, lime juice, red pepper flakes (optional), salt, and pepper.
7. Pour the sauce over the shrimp and vegetables in the pan and toss to coat evenly.
8. Add the cooked rice noodles to the pan and stir-fry for an additional 2 minutes to heat through.
9. Adjust the seasoning if needed.
10. Remove the shrimp stir-fry from the heat and serve hot as a flavorful and satisfying dinner.
- **Estimated time: 30 minutes**
- **Nutritional information (per serving):** Calories: 350 - Protein: 18g
- Fat: 7g - Carbohydrates: 55g
- **Shopping list:**
- Rice noodles, shrimp, mixed vegetables (e.g., bell peppers, broccoli, carrots, snap peas), garlic cloves, ginger, soy sauce (gluten-free if needed), sesame oil, lime juice, red pepper flakes (optional), salt, pepper

Shrimp Stir-Fry with Rice Noodles

# DAIRY-FREE RECIPES

## Coconut Milk Smoothie

**Ingredients:**

- 1 cup coconut milk
- 1 ripe banana
- 1 cup mixed berries (such as strawberries, blueberries, or raspberries)
- 1 tablespoon honey or maple syrup (optional)
- Ice cubes (optional)

**Estimated Time: 5 minutes**

**Nutritional Information (per serving):**

- Calories: 250 Protein: 3g
- Fat: 15g Carbohydrates: 30g

**Instructions:**

1. In a blender, combine the coconut milk, ripe banana, mixed berries, and sweetener (if using).
2. Blend until smooth and creamy.
3. Add ice cubes if desired and blend again until well combined.
4. Pour into glasses and serve immediately.

**Shopping List:**- Coconut milk - Ripe banana

- Mixed berries (strawberries, blueberries, raspberries)

- Honey or maple syrup (optional) - Ice cubes (optional)

# Vegan Spinach and Mushroom Frittata

## Ingredients:

- 1 tablespoon olive oil
- 1 small onion, diced
- 2 cloves garlic, minced
- 2 cups sliced mushrooms
- 2 cups fresh spinach
- 1 cup chickpea flour
- 1 cup unsweetened almond milk
- 2 tablespoons nutritional yeast
- 1 teaspoon dried thyme
- Salt and pepper to taste

## Estimated Time: 35 minutes

## Nutritional Information (per serving):

- Calories: 200
- Protein: 9g
- Fat: 10g
- Carbohydrates: 20g

## Instructions:

1. Preheat the oven to 375°F (190°C).
2. In a skillet, heat the olive oil over medium heat.
3. Add the diced onion and minced garlic to the skillet and sauté until softened and fragrant.
4. Add the sliced mushrooms and cook until they release their moisture and become tender.
5. Add the fresh spinach and cook until wilted.

6. In a bowl, whisk together the chickpea flour, almond milk, nutritional yeast, dried thyme, salt, and pepper.
7. Pour the chickpea flour mixture over the sautéed vegetables in the skillet and stir well to combine.
8. Transfer the skillet to the preheated oven and bake for 20-25 minutes until the frittata is set and golden brown on top.
9. Remove from the oven and let it cool slightly before slicing and serving.

**Shopping List:**

- Olive oil
- Small onion
- Garlic cloves
- Sliced mushrooms
- Fresh spinach
- Chickpea flour
- Unsweetened almond milk
- Nutritional yeast
- Dried thyme
- Salt
- Pepper

# Cashew Cheese Stuffed Peppers

## Ingredients:

- 4 bell peppers (any color)
- 1 cup raw cashews, soaked in water for 4 hours and drained
- 2 tablespoons nutritional yeast
- 1 tablespoon lemon juice
- 1 clove garlic, minced
- 1/4 teaspoon salt
- 1/4 teaspoon pepper
- Fresh basil leaves, for garnish

**Estimated Time: 50 minutes**

**Nutritional Information (per serving):**

- Calories: 250
- Protein: 8g
- Fat: 15g
- Carbohydrates: 25g

## Instructions:

1. Preheat the oven to 375°F (190°C).
2. Cut off pepper tops and remove seeds/membranes. Set aside.
3. In a food processor or blender, combine the soaked cashews, nutritional yeast, lemon juice, minced garlic, salt, and pepper. Blend until smooth and creamy.

4. Spoon the cashew cheese mixture into the hollowed-out bell peppers, filling them to the top.
5. Put stuffed peppers in a baking dish, and cover with foil.
6. Bake in the preheated oven for 30 minutes.
7. Remove the foil and continue baking for an additional 10 minutes until the peppers are tender and the cheese is slightly golden.
8. Garnish with fresh basil leaves before serving.

## Shopping List:

- Bell peppers
- Raw cashews
- Nutritional yeast
- Lemon juice
- Garlic clove
- Salt
- Pepper
- Fresh basil leaves

# Dairy-Free Chocolate Avocado Mousse

**Ingredients:**

- 2 ripe avocados

- 1/4 cup unsweetened cocoa powder

- 1/4 cup maple syrup or agave nectar

- 1/4 cup unsweetened almond milk

- 1 teaspoon vanilla extract

- Pinch of salt

- Fresh berries, for garnish

**Estimated Time: 10 minutes**

**Nutritional Information (per serving):**

- Calories: 200
- Protein: 3g
- Fat: 15g
- Carbohydrates: 20g

**Instructions:**

1. Cut the avocados in half, remove the pits, and scoop the flesh into a blender or food processor.
2. Add the cocoa powder, maple syrup or agave nectar, almond milk, vanilla extract, and salt to the blender.
3. Blend until smooth and creamy, scraping down the sides as needed.
4. Divide the mousse into serving dishes or glasses.

5. Chill in the refrigerator for at least 1 hour to set.
6. Garnish with fresh berries before serving.

## Shopping List:

- Ripe avocados
- Unsweetened cocoa powder
- Maple syrup or agave nectar
- Unsweetened almond milk
- Vanilla extract
- Salt
- Fresh berries

# Vegan Lentil Curry with Brown Rice

**Ingredients:**

- 1 cup brown lentils, rinsed and drained
- 1 tablespoon olive oil
- 1 onion, diced
- 2 cloves garlic, minced
- 1 tablespoon curry powder
- 1 teaspoon ground cumin
- 1 teaspoon ground coriander
- 1/2 teaspoon turmeric
- 1/4 teaspoon cayenne pepper (optional)
- 1 can (14 ounces) diced tomatoes
- 1 can (14 ounces) of coconut milk
- 2 cups vegetable broth
- Salt and pepper to taste
- Cooked brown rice, for serving
- Fresh cilantro, for garnish

**Estimated Time: 45 minutes**

**Nutritional Information (per serving):**

- Calories: 350 - Protein: 15g

- Fat: 10g - Carbohydrates: 50g

**Instructions:**

1. In a large pot, heat the olive oil over medium heat.
2. Add the diced onion and minced garlic to the pot and sauté until softened and fragrant.

3. Add the curry powder, ground cumin, ground coriander, turmeric, and cayenne pepper (if using) to the pot. Stir well to coat the onions and garlic with the spices.
4. Add the rinsed and drained lentils, diced tomatoes, coconut milk, and vegetable broth to the pot. Stir to combine.
5. Bring the mixture to a boil, then reduce the heat to low. Cover the pot and simmer for 30-35 minutes until the lentils are tender and the flavors have melded together.
6. Season with salt and pepper to taste.
7. Serve the lentil curry over cooked brown rice and garnish with fresh cilantro.

**Shopping List:**

- Brown lentils, Olive oil
- Onion
- Garlic cloves
- Curry powder
- Ground cumin
- Ground coriander
- Turmeric
- Cayenne pepper (optional)
- Diced tomatoes (canned)
- Coconut milk (canned)
- Vegetable broth
- Salt, Pepper
- Cooked brown rice, Fresh cilantro

# Almond Milk Chia Pudding

**Ingredients:**

- 1/4 cup chia seeds

- 1 cup unsweetened almond milk

- 1 tablespoon maple syrup or agave nectar

- 1/2 teaspoon vanilla extract

- Fresh fruit, nuts, or seeds for topping (optional)

**Estimated Time: 5 minutes + overnight chilling**

**Nutritional Information (per serving):**

- Calories: 180
- Protein: 5g
- Fat: 10g
- Carbohydrates: 18g

**Instructions:**

1. In a bowl, combine the chia seeds, unsweetened almond milk, maple syrup or agave nectar, and vanilla extract. Stir well to combine.
2. Cover the bowl and refrigerate overnight or for at least 4 hours to allow the chia seeds to absorb the liquid and thicken.
3. Stir the chia pudding before serving to ensure it is well-mixed and creamy.
4. Serve the chia pudding in individual bowls or glasses and top with fresh fruit, nuts, or seeds if desired.

**Shopping List:**

- Chia seeds

- Unsweetened almond milk

- Maple syrup or agave nectar

- Vanilla extract

- Fresh fruit, nuts, or seeds (optional)

# Roasted Vegetable Quinoa Bowl with Tahini Dressing

**Ingredients:**

- 1 cup quinoa, rinsed
- 2 cups vegetable broth
- 1 small sweet potato, peeled and diced
- 1 red bell pepper, seeded and diced
- 1 zucchini, diced
- 1 cup cherry tomatoes, halved
- 1 tablespoon olive oil
- Salt and pepper to taste
- 1/4 cup tahini
- 1 tablespoon lemon juice
- 2 tablespoons water
- 1 clove garlic, minced
- Fresh parsley or cilantro, for garnish

**Estimated Time: 40 minutes**

**Nutritional Information (per serving):**

- Calories: 350
- Protein: 10g
- Fat: 12g
- Carbohydrates: 50g

## Instructions:

1. Preheat the oven to 400°F (200°C).
2. In a saucepan, combine the quinoa and vegetable broth. Bring to a boil, then reduce the heat to low, cover, and simmer for about 15-20 minutes until the quinoa is tender and the liquid is absorbed.
3. On a separate baking sheet, toss the diced sweet potato, red bell pepper, zucchini, and cherry tomatoes with olive oil, salt, and pepper.
4. Roast the vegetables in the preheated oven for about 20-25 minutes until they are tender and slightly caramelized.
5. In a small bowl, whisk together the tahini, lemon juice, water, and minced garlic until smooth and creamy. Add more water if needed to reach desired consistency.
6. To assemble the quinoa bowls, divide the cooked quinoa among serving bowls. Top with the roasted vegetables and drizzle with the tahini dressing.
7. Garnish with fresh parsley or cilantro before serving.

## Shopping List:

- Quinoa, Vegetable broth
- Small sweet potato
- Red bell pepper
- Zucchini
- Cherry tomatoes
- Olive oil, Salt, and Pepper
- Tahini, Lemon juice
- Garlic clove, Fresh parsley, or cilantro

# PESCETARIAN RECIPES

## Grilled Salmon with Lemon-Dill Sauce

**Ingredients:**

- 4 salmon fillets
- 2 tablespoons olive oil
- Salt and pepper to taste
- 2 tablespoons fresh dill, chopped
- Juice of 1 lemon
- 1/4 cup plain Greek yogurt

**Estimated Time: 20 minutes**

**Nutritional Information (per serving):**

- Calories: 300
- Protein: 30g
- Fat: 18g
- Carbohydrates: 2g

**Instructions:**

1. Preheat the grill to medium-high heat.
2. Coat the salmon fillets in a generous layer of olive oil and sprinkle with a pinch of salt and pepper.
3. Place the salmon fillets on the grill, skin-side down, and cook for about 4-5 minutes per side or until the salmon is cooked through and flakes easily with a fork.

4. In a small bowl, mix the chopped dill, lemon juice, and Greek yogurt to make the lemon-dill sauce.
5. Serve the grilled salmon with the lemon-dill sauce on the side.

**Shopping List:**

- Salmon fillets
- Olive oil
- Salt
- Pepper
- Fresh dill
- Lemon
- Plain Greek yogurt

# Tuna Poke Bowl

## Ingredients:

- 1 cup sushi rice, cooked
- 1/2 pound fresh tuna, cubed
- 1/4 cup soy sauce
- 1 tablespoon sesame oil
- 1 tablespoon rice vinegar
- 1 tablespoon honey
- 1 teaspoon grated ginger
- 1/2 avocado, sliced
- 1/2 cucumber, sliced
- 1/4 cup edamame beans, steamed
- 1/4 cup sliced radishes
- Nori seaweed, cut into thin strips (optional)
- Sesame seeds, for garnish
- Green onions, chopped, for garnish

## Estimated Time: 30 minutes

## Nutritional Information (per serving):

- Calories: 450
- Protein: 30g
- Fat: 15g
- Carbohydrates: 45g

## Instructions:

1. In a bowl, combine the soy sauce, sesame oil, rice vinegar, honey, and grated ginger to make the marinade.

2. Combine the cubed tuna with the marinade, ensuring each piece is thoroughly coated Place the mixture in the refrigerator and allow it to marinate for a period of 15 to 20 minutes.
3. In a serving bowl, arrange the cooked sushi rice as the base.
4. Top the rice with marinated tuna, sliced avocado, sliced cucumber, steamed edamame beans, and sliced radishes.
5. Garnish with nori seaweed, sesame seeds, and chopped green onions.
6. Serve the tuna poke bowl immediately.

**Shopping List:**

- Sushi rice
- Fresh tuna
- Soy sauce
- Sesame oil
- Rice vinegar
- Honey
- Ginger
- Avocado
- Cucumber
- Edamame beans
- Radishes
- Nori seaweed (optional)
- Sesame seeds
- Green onions

# Garlic Shrimp Stir-Fry with Vegetables

## Ingredients:

- 1 pound shrimp, peeled and deveined
- 2 tablespoons olive oil
- 4 cloves garlic, minced
- 1 red bell pepper, sliced
- 1 yellow bell pepper, sliced
- 1 zucchini, sliced
- 1 cup snap peas
- 2 tablespoons soy sauce
- 1 tablespoon honey
- 1 teaspoon cornstarch
- Salt and pepper to taste
- Fresh cilantro, for garnish (optional)
- Cooked rice or noodles, for serving

**Estimated Time: 25 minutes**

**Nutritional Information (per serving):**

- Calories: 300
- Protein: 25g
- Fat: 12g
- Carbohydrates: 20g

## Instructions:

1. Heat the olive oil in a large skillet or wok over medium-high heat.

2. Once the oil is hot, add the minced garlic to the skillet and sauté for approximately 1 minute, or until the garlic becomes fragrant.
3. Add the shrimp to the skillet and cook for about 2-3 minutes until pink and cooked through. Carefully take out the shrimp from the skillet and set them aside for now.
4. In the same skillet, add the sliced bell peppers, zucchini, and snap peas. Stir-fry for about 5 minutes until the vegetables are crisp-tender.
5. In a small bowl, whisk together the soy sauce, honey, and cornstarch to make the sauce.
6. Pour the sauce into the skillet with the vegetables and cook for 1-2 minutes until the sauce thickens.
7. Return the cooked shrimp to the skillet and toss to coat everything in the sauce.
8. Season with salt and pepper to taste.
9. Garnish with fresh cilantro, if desired.
10. Serve the garlic shrimp stir-fry over cooked rice or noodles.

## Shopping List:

- Shrimp, Olive oil
- Garlic, Red bell pepper
- Yellow bell pepper - Zucchini - Snap peas - Soy sauce - Honey – Cornstarch – Salt – Pepper - Fresh cilantro - Cooked rice or noodles

# Baked Cod with Mediterranean Salsa

## Ingredients:

- 4 cod fillets
- 2 tablespoons olive oil
- Salt and pepper to taste
- 1 cup cherry tomatoes, halved
- 1/2 cup kalamata olives, pitted and chopped
- 1/4 cup diced red onion
- 1/4 cup chopped fresh parsley
- 1 tablespoon lemon juice
- 1 tablespoon balsamic vinegar

## Estimated Time: 30 minutes

## Nutritional Information (per serving):

- Calories: 250
- Protein: 30g
- Fat: 12g
- Carbohydrates: 6g

## Instructions:

1. Preheat the oven to 400°F (200°C).
2. Arrange the cod fillets on a baking sheet that has been lined with parchment paper.
3. Drizzle the cod fillets with olive oil and season with salt and pepper.
4. Bake the cod in the preheated oven for about 15-20 minutes until cooked through and flaky.

5. As the cod bakes, begin preparing the Mediterranean salsa. In a bowl, combine the cherry tomatoes, kalamata olives, diced red onion, chopped fresh parsley, lemon juice, and balsamic vinegar. Toss to combine.
6. Remove the cod from the oven and serve it with the Mediterranean salsa spooned over the top.

## Shopping List:

- Cod fillets
- Olive oil
- Salt
- Pepper
- Cherry tomatoes
- Kalamata olives
- Red onion
- Fresh parsley
- Lemon
- Balsamic vinegar

# Zucchini and Salmon Cakes

**Ingredients:**

- 2 cups grated zucchini
- 1/2 pound fresh salmon fillet, cooked and flaked
- 1/4 cup breadcrumbs
- 2 green onions, chopped
- 1/4 cup chopped fresh dill
- 1 egg, beaten
- Salt and pepper to taste
- 2 tablespoons olive oil

**Estimated Time: 35 minutes**

**Nutritional Information (per serving):**

- Calories: 200
- Protein: 15g
- Fat: 10g
- Carbohydrates: 10g

**Instructions:**

1. Transfer the grated zucchini to a colander and sprinkle it with a pinch of salt. Let it sit for 10 minutes to release excess moisture. Squeeze out any remaining moisture from the zucchini using a clean kitchen towel or paper towel.
2. In a large bowl, combine the grated zucchini, flaked salmon, breadcrumbs, chopped green onions, chopped fresh dill, beaten egg, salt, and pepper. Mix until well combined.

3. Shape the mixture into patties.
4. In a skillet, heat the olive oil over medium heat.
5. Cook the zucchini and salmon cakes in the skillet for about 4-5 minutes per side until golden brown and cooked through.
6. Serve the zucchini and salmon cakes with a side salad or your favorite dipping sauce.

## Shopping List:

- Zucchini
- Fresh salmon fillet
- Breadcrumbs
- Green onions
- Fresh dill
- Egg
- Salt
- Pepper
- Olive oil

# Greek Style Grilled Fish Skewers

## Ingredients:

- 1 pound white fish fillets (such as halibut or cod), cut into chunks
- 1/4 cup olive oil
- Juice of 1 lemon
- 2 cloves garlic, minced
- 1 teaspoon dried oregano
- Salt and pepper to taste
- Cherry tomatoes
- Red onion, cut into chunks
- Lemon wedges, for serving

## Estimated Time: 25 minutes

## Nutritional Information (per serving):

- Calories: 250
- Protein: 30g
- Fat: 12g
- Carbohydrates: 6g

## 1. Instructions:

1. Combine the olive oil, lemon juice, minced garlic, dried oregano, salt, and pepper in a bowl. Whisk them together until they form a marinade.
2. Add the fish chunks to the marinade and toss to coat. Place the mixture in the refrigerator and allow it to marinate for a period of 15 to 20 minutes.
3. Preheat the grill to medium-high heat.

4. Thread the marinated fish chunks onto skewers, alternating with cherry tomatoes and chunks of red onion.
5. Grill the fish skewers for about 4-5 minutes per side or until the fish is cooked through and flakes easily with a fork.
6. Serve the grilled fish skewers with lemon wedges on the side.

**Shopping List:**

- White fish fillets (halibut or cod)
- Olive oil
- Lemon
- Garlic
- Dried oregano
- Salt
- Pepper
- Cherry tomatoes
- Red onion
- Lemon wedges

# Shrimp and Quinoa Stuffed Bell Peppers

**Ingredients:**

- 4 bell peppers
- 1 cup cooked quinoa
- 1/2 pound shrimp, peeled and deveined
- 1 tablespoon olive oil
- 1/2 onion, chopped
- 2 cloves garlic, minced
- 1 zucchini, diced
- 1 cup cherry tomatoes, halved
- 1/4 cup chopped fresh parsley
- 1/4 cup crumbled feta cheese
- Salt and pepper to taste

**Estimated Time: 45 minutes**

**Nutritional Information (per serving):**

- Calories: 300
- Protein: 25g
- Fat: 10g
- Carbohydrates: 30g

**Instructions:**

1. Preheat the oven to 375°F (190°C).
2. Cut off pepper tops and remove seeds/membranes. Set aside.
3. In a skillet, heat the olive oil over medium heat.
4. Add the chopped onion and minced garlic to the skillet and sauté until softened and fragrant.

5. Add the diced zucchini and cook for another 3-4 minutes until slightly tender.
6. Place the shrimp in the heated skillet and cook them for approximately 2 to 3 minutes, or until they turn pink and are fully cooked. Remove from heat.
7. In a bowl, combine the cooked quinoa, cooked shrimp mixture, cherry tomatoes, chopped fresh parsley, crumbled feta cheese, salt, and pepper. Mix well.
8. Spoon the quinoa and shrimp mixture into the hollowed-out bell peppers.
9. Place the stuffed bell peppers on a baking sheet and bake in the preheated oven for 25-30 minutes until the peppers are tender and the filling is heated through.
10. Serve the shrimp and quinoa stuffed bell peppers as a main dish.

## Shopping List:

- Bell peppers
- Quinoa
- Shrimp - Olive oil
- Onion – Garlic - Zucchini
- Cherry tomatoes - Fresh parsley - Feta cheese
- Salt
- Pepper

# Pescetarian Sushi Rolls

## Ingredients:

- 4 nori seaweed sheets
- 2 cups cooked sushi rice
- Assorted vegetables (such as cucumber, avocado, carrots, and bell peppers), sliced into thin strips
- Assorted seafood (such as cooked shrimp, crab, smoked salmon, and tuna), sliced into thin strips
- Soy sauce, for serving
- Wasabi, for serving
- Pickled ginger, for serving

**Estimated Time: 30 minutes**

**Nutritional Information (per serving):**

- Calories: 250
- Protein: 10g
- Fat: 5g
- Carbohydrates: 45g

## Instructions:

1. Place a nori seaweed sheet on a bamboo sushi mat or a sheet of plastic wrap.
2. Moisten your hands with water to prevent the rice from sticking. Spread about 1/2 cup of sushi rice evenly on the nori seaweed, leaving a 1-inch border at the top.
3. Arrange the vegetable and seafood strips on top of the rice, slightly towards the bottom.

4. Using the sushi mat or plastic wrap, tightly roll the nori seaweed, rice, and fillings into a compact cylinder shape.
5. Dampen a sharp knife with water and use it to slice the sushi roll into bite-sized pieces.
6. Repeat the process with the remaining nori seaweed sheets, rice, and fillings.
7. Serve the pescetarian sushi rolls with soy sauce, wasabi, and pickled ginger.

## Shopping List:

- Nori seaweed sheets
- Sushi rice
- Assorted vegetables (cucumber, avocado, carrots, bell peppers)
- Assorted seafood (shrimp, crab, smoked salmon, tuna)
- Soy sauce
- Wasabi
- Pickled ginger

# VEGAN RECIPES

## Chickpea Curry with Coconut Milk

**Ingredients:**

- 1 tablespoon olive oil
- 1 onion, diced
- 3 cloves garlic, minced
- 1 tablespoon curry powder
- 1 teaspoon ground cumin
- 1 teaspoon ground coriander
- 1 can (15 ounces) chickpeas, drained and rinsed
- 1 can (14 ounces) diced tomatoes
- 1 can (14 ounces) of coconut milk
- 1 cup vegetable broth
- Salt and pepper to taste
- Fresh cilantro, for garnish (optional)
- Cooked rice or naan bread, for serving

**Estimated Time: 30 minutes**

**Nutritional Information (per serving):**

- Calories: 380  - Protein: 12g

- Fat: 20g - Carbohydrates: 41g

**Instructions:**

1. Heat the olive oil in a large pot or skillet over medium heat.
2. Add the diced onion and minced garlic to the pot and sauté until the onion is translucent and fragrant.

3. Stir in the curry powder, ground cumin, and ground coriander, and cook for an additional minute to toast the spices.
4. Add the chickpeas, diced tomatoes, coconut milk, and vegetable broth to the pot.
5. Season with salt and pepper to taste.
6. Bring the mixture to a simmer and let it cook for about 20 minutes, allowing the flavors to meld together.
7. Serve the chickpea curry either over cooked rice or alongside naan bread.
8. Garnish with fresh cilantro, if desired.

## Shopping List:

- Olive oil - Onion
- Garlic - Curry powder
- Ground cumin - Ground coriander
- Canned chickpeas - Canned diced tomatoes
- Canned coconut milk - Vegetable broth
- Salt – Pepper - Fresh cilantro (optional)
- Cooked rice or naan bread

# Vegan Lentil Bolognese with Zucchini Noodles

**Ingredients:**

- 2 tablespoons olive oil
- 1 onion, diced
- 3 cloves garlic, minced
- 1 carrot, diced
- 1 stalk celery, diced
- 1 red bell pepper, diced
- 1 cup dried green or brown lentils, rinsed
- 1 can (14 ounces) crushed tomatoes
- 1 tablespoon tomato paste
- 1 teaspoon dried oregano
- 1 teaspoon dried basil
- Salt and pepper to taste
- Zucchini noodles (zoodles), for serving
- Fresh basil, for garnish (optional)

**Estimated Time: 45 minutes**

**Nutritional Information (per serving):**

- Calories: 320

- Protein: 15g

- Fat: 8g

- Carbohydrates: 48g

## Instructions:

1. Heat the olive oil in a large pot or skillet over medium heat.
2. Add the diced onion and minced garlic to the pot and sauté until the onion is translucent and fragrant.
3. Add the diced carrot, celery, and red bell pepper to the pot. Cook until the vegetables are slightly softened.
4. Stir in the rinsed lentils, crushed tomatoes, tomato paste, dried oregano, and dried basil.
5. Season with salt and pepper to taste.
6. Bring the mixture to a boil, then reduce the heat to low and let it simmer for about 30 minutes or until the lentils are cooked and the sauce has thickened.
7. Serve the lentil bolognese over zucchini noodles (zoodles).
8. Garnish with fresh basil, if desired.

## Shopping List:

- Olive oil – Onion - Garlic - Carrot
- Celery - Red bell pepper
- Dried green or brown lentils
- Canned crushed tomatoes
- Tomato paste - Dried oregano - Dried basil
- Salt - Pepper
- Zucchini - Fresh basil (optional)

# Roasted Vegetable Quinoa Salad

## Ingredients:

- 1 cup quinoa
- 2 cups water
- 1 red bell pepper, diced
- 1 yellow bell pepper, diced
- 1 zucchini, diced
- 1 eggplant, diced
- 1 red onion, sliced
- 2 tablespoons olive oil
- 1 teaspoon dried thyme
- Salt and pepper to taste
- 2 tablespoons lemon juice
- 2 tablespoons balsamic vinegar
- 1/4 cup chopped fresh parsley
- 1/4 cup chopped fresh basil
- 1/4 cup chopped fresh mint

**Estimated Time: 40 minutes**

**Nutritional Information (per serving):**

- Calories: 310 - Protein: 8g

- Fat: 12g- Carbohydrates: 45g

## Instructions:

1. Preheat the oven to 400°F (200°C).
2. Rinse the quinoa under cold water.
3. In a saucepan, combine the quinoa and water. Bring to a boil, then reduce the heat to low, cover,

and let it simmer for about 15 minutes or until the quinoa is tender and the water is absorbed. Fluff with a fork and set aside.

4. In a large baking dish, combine the diced red and yellow bell peppers, zucchini, eggplant, and sliced red onion.

5. Drizzle the mixture with olive oil and sprinkle it with dried thyme, salt, and pepper. Toss to coat the vegetables evenly.

6. Roast the vegetables in the preheated oven for about 25 minutes or until they are tender and slightly browned, stirring once halfway through.

7. In a small bowl, whisk together the lemon juice and balsamic vinegar to make the dressing.

8. In a large serving bowl, combine the cooked quinoa, roasted vegetables, chopped fresh parsley, basil, and mint.

9. Pour the dressing evenly over the salad and toss everything together to ensure all ingredients are coated.

10. Serve the roasted vegetable quinoa salad warm or at room temperature.

**Shopping List:** - Quinoa

- Red bell pepper - Yellow bell pepper
- Zucchini - Eggplant
- Red onion - Olive oil- Dried thyme - Salt
- Pepper - Lemon juice- Balsamic vinegar
- Fresh parsley  - Fresh basil- Fresh mint

# Vegan Black Bean Burgers

**Ingredients:**

- 1 can (15 ounces) of black beans, drained and rinsed
- 1/2 cup cooked quinoa
- 1/2 cup breadcrumbs (gluten-free if desired)
- 1/4 cup diced onion
- 2 cloves garlic, minced
- 1 teaspoon ground cumin
- 1 teaspoon paprika
- Salt and pepper to taste
- 1 tablespoon olive oil
- Burger buns, for serving
- Lettuce, tomato slices, and other desired toppings

**Estimated Time: 30 minutes**

**Nutritional Information (per serving):**

- Calories: 280
- Protein: 12g
- Fat: 6g
- Carbohydrates: 47g

**Instructions:**

1. In a mixing bowl, mash the black beans with a fork or potato masher until mostly mashed but with some whole beans remaining.
2. Add the cooked quinoa, breadcrumbs, diced onion, minced garlic, ground cumin, paprika, salt, and

pepper to the bowl. Mix well to combine all the ingredients.

3. Divide the mixture into 4 equal portions, then shape each portion into a patty.
4. In a skillet, heat the olive oil over medium heat.
5. Cook the black bean patties in the skillet for about 4-5 minutes on each side or until they are heated through and slightly crispy on the outside.
6. Serve the vegan black bean burgers on burger buns and top with lettuce, tomato slices, and any other desired toppings.

**Shopping List:**

- Canned black beans - Cooked quinoa
- Breadcrumbs (gluten-free if desired)
- Onion – Garlic - Ground cumin
- Paprika – Salt – Pepper - Olive oil
- Burger buns - Lettuce
- Tomato

# Sweet Potato and Chickpea Coconut Curry

**Ingredients:**

- 1 tablespoon coconut oil
- 1 onion, diced
- 3 cloves garlic, minced
- 1 tablespoon curry powder
- 1 teaspoon ground cumin
- 1 teaspoon ground coriander
- 1 sweet potato, peeled and diced
- 1 can (15 ounces) chickpeas, drained and rinsed
- 1 can (14 ounces) diced tomatoes
- 1 can (14 ounces) of coconut milk
- 1 cup vegetable broth
- Salt and pepper to taste
- Fresh cilantro, for garnish (optional)
- Cooked rice or naan bread, for serving

**Estimated Time: 45 minutes**

**Nutritional Information (per serving):**

- Calories: 380
- Protein: 10g
- Fat: 15g
- Carbohydrates: 55g

**Instructions:**

1. Heat the coconut oil in a large pot or skillet over medium heat.

2. Add the diced onion and minced garlic to the pot and sauté until the onion is translucent and fragrant.
3. Stir in the curry powder, ground cumin, and ground coriander, and cook for an additional minute to toast the spices.
4. Add the diced sweet potato, drained and rinsed chickpeas, diced tomatoes, coconut milk, and vegetable broth to the pot.
5. Season with salt and pepper to taste.
6. Bring the mixture to a simmer and let it cook for about 30 minutes or until the sweet potatoes are tender.
7. Serve the sweet potato and chickpea coconut curry over cooked rice or with naan bread.
8. Garnish with fresh cilantro, if desired.

**Shopping List:**

- Coconut oil
- Onion - Garlic
- Curry powder - Ground cumin
- Ground coriander - Sweet potato
- Canned chickpeas - Canned diced tomatoes
- Canned coconut milk - Vegetable broth
- Salt – Pepper - Fresh cilantro (optional)
- Cooked rice or naan bread

# Vegan Pad Thai with Tofu

**Ingredients:**

- 8 ounces of rice noodles
- 2 tablespoons soy sauce
- 1 tablespoon maple syrup
- 1 tablespoon lime juice
- 2 tablespoons vegetable oil
- 1 onion, thinly sliced
- 3 cloves garlic, minced
- 1 red bell pepper, thinly sliced
- 1 carrot, julienned
- 1 cup bean sprouts
- 1 cup tofu, cubed
- Chopped peanuts, for garnish (optional)
- Chopped cilantro, for garnish (optional)
- Lime wedges, for serving

**Estimated Time: 30 minutes**

**Nutritional Information (per serving):**

- Calories: 450
- Protein: 12g
- Fat: 15g
- Carbohydrates: 70g

1. **Instructions:**

1. Cook rice noodles as per package instructions. Drain and set aside.
2. In a small bowl, whisk together the soy sauce, maple syrup, and lime juice to make the sauce. Set aside.

3. Heat the vegetable oil in a large skillet or wok over medium heat.
4. Add the thinly sliced onion and minced garlic to the skillet and sauté until the onion is translucent and fragrant.
5. Add the sliced red bell pepper, julienned carrot, and cubed tofu to the skillet. Stir-fry for about 5-6 minutes or until the vegetables are tender.
6. Add the cooked rice noodles to the skillet, followed by the sauce. Toss everything together to coat the noodles and vegetables evenly with the sauce.
7. Cook for an additional 2-3 minutes to heat everything through.
8. Serve the vegan pad Thai garnished with chopped peanuts and cilantro, if desired. Serve with lime wedges on the side.

**Shopping List:**

- Rice noodles - Soy sauce
- Maple syrup - Lime juice
- Vegetable oil - Onion
- Garlic - Red bell pepper
- Carrot - Bean sprouts
- Tofu - Chopped peanuts (optional)
- Chopped cilantro (optional)
- Lime wedges

# Spicy Vegan Chili with Quinoa

## Ingredients:

- 1 tablespoon olive oil
- 1 onion, diced
- 3 cloves garlic, minced
- 1 red bell pepper, diced
- 1 green bell pepper, diced
- 1 jalapeno pepper, seeded and minced
- 1 can (15 ounces) of kidney beans, drained and rinsed
- 1 can (15 ounces) of black beans, drained and rinsed
- 1 can (14 ounces) diced tomatoes
- 1 can (6 ounces) tomato paste
- 2 cups vegetable broth
- 1 cup cooked quinoa
- 1 tablespoon chili powder
- 1 teaspoon cumin
- 1 teaspoon paprika
- Salt and pepper to taste
- Fresh cilantro, for garnish (optional)
- Sliced avocado, for serving (optional)

**Estimated Time: 45 minutes**

**Nutritional Information (per serving):**

- Calories: 360 - Protein: 15g
- Fat: 6g - Carbohydrates: 65g

## Instructions:

1. Heat the olive oil in a large pot or Dutch oven over medium heat.
2. Add the diced onion, minced garlic, diced red bell pepper, diced green bell pepper, and minced jalapeno pepper to the pot. Sauté until the vegetables are softened.
3. Stir in the drained and rinsed kidney beans, drained and rinsed black beans, diced tomatoes, tomato paste, vegetable broth, cooked quinoa, chili powder, cumin, paprika, salt, and pepper.
4. Bring the chili to a simmer and let it cook for about 30 minutes to allow the flavors to meld together.
5. Serve the spicy vegan chili garnished with fresh cilantro, if desired. Serve with sliced avocado on the side.

## Shopping List:

- Olive oil – Onion - Garlic
- Red bell pepper - Green bell pepper
- Jalapeno pepper - Canned kidney beans
- Canned black beans - Canned diced tomatoes
- Canned tomato paste - Vegetable broth
- Cooked quinoa - Chili powder
- Cumin – Paprika – Salt - Pepper
- Fresh cilantro (optional)
- Avocado (optional)

# Vegan Mango Coconut Chia Pudding

**Ingredients:**

- 1/4 cup chia seeds
- 1 cup coconut milk
- 1 ripe mango, peeled and chopped
- 1 tablespoon maple syrup (optional)
- Fresh mint leaves, for garnish (optional)

**Estimated Time: 5 minutes (plus chilling time)**

**Nutritional Information (per serving):**

- Calories: 280
- Protein: 5g
- Fat: 16g
- Carbohydrates: 30g

**Instructions:**

1. Combine the chia seeds and coconut milk in a bowl. Stirring well to ensure the chia seeds are evenly distributed and fully submerged in the liquid.
2. Place a cover or lid on the bowl, then refrigerate it for a minimum of 2 hours, or ideally overnight. This duration allows the chia seeds to absorb the liquid and create a thickened consistency.
3. Once the chia pudding has thickened, remove it from the refrigerator.
4. Place the chopped mango in a blender and blend it until it reaches a smooth consistency.

5. Sweeten the mango puree with maple syrup, if desired.
6. Layer the chia pudding and mango puree in serving glasses or bowls.
7. Garnish with fresh mint leaves, if desired.
8. Serve the vegan mango coconut chia pudding chilled.

**Shopping List:**

- Chia seeds
- Coconut milk
- Ripe mango
- Maple syrup (optional)
- Fresh mint leaves (optional)

Sweet Potato Hash with Eggs

Mexican Stuffed Bell Peppers with Brown Rice

# CONCLUSION

In conclusion, adopting a specialized diet and making lifestyle changes can be instrumental in managing Hashimoto's disease. The recipes and meal plans provided in "Hashimoto's Diet for Beginners: A Cookbook with 100 Quick, Easy, and Delicious Recipes for Thyroid Healing and a 30-Day Meal Plan" offers a variety of options that are both nourishing and enjoyable.

By following the guidance in this book, individuals with Hashimoto's disease can take control of their health and improve their overall well-being.

## Tips for Managing Hashimoto's Disease Through Diet and Lifestyle Changes

1. Consult with a healthcare professional: It is essential to work closely with a healthcare professional, such as a registered dietitian or endocrinologist, who specializes in Hashimoto's disease. They can offer customized recommendations and guidance that are specifically tailored to your unique needs and preferences.

2. Eliminate trigger foods: Certain foods can trigger inflammation and exacerbate Hashimoto's symptoms. Common triggers include gluten, dairy, and processed foods. Consider eliminating these foods from your diet and monitor how your body responds.

3. Emphasize nutrient-dense foods: Focus on consuming nutrient-dense foods that support thyroid health. This includes incorporating plenty of fresh fruits and vegetables, lean proteins, healthy fats, and whole grains into your meals.

4. Balance your macronutrients: Aim to balance your macronutrients, including carbohydrates, proteins, and fats, to provide sustained energy and support your body's functions. Include a variety of these nutrients in each meal and snack

5. Prioritize gut health: The health of your gut can impact your overall well-being, including Hashimoto's disease. Incorporate probiotic-rich foods like yogurt, sauerkraut, and kefir, as well as fiber-rich foods like fruits, vegetables, and whole grains, to support a healthy gut microbiome.

6. Manage stress: Stress can contribute to Hashimoto's symptoms. Implement stress management techniques such as meditation, yoga, deep breathing exercises, and regular physical activity to help reduce stress levels.

7. Get enough sleep: Adequate sleep is crucial for hormone regulation and overall health. Create a

regular sleep routine and strive to obtain 7-9 hours of restful sleep every night.

## Resources for People with Hashimoto's Disease

1.  Books and Websites: Explore additional resources on Hashimoto's disease, including reputable books and websites that provide in-depth information and practical tips for managing the condition. Some recommended resources include "The Hashimoto's Protocol" by Izabella Wentz and the American Thyroid Association website.

2.  Support Groups: Join local or online support groups to connect with others who have Hashimoto's disease. These groups can provide valuable insights, support, and encouragement throughout your journey.

3.  Professional Guidance: Consider working with a registered dietitian, naturopathic doctor, or functional medicine practitioner who specializes in autoimmune conditions. They can provide personalized guidance, tailored meal plans, and ongoing support to help you navigate your dietary needs.

Remember, managing Hashimoto's disease requires a holistic approach that combines a healthy diet, lifestyle modifications, and medical guidance. By incorporating the recipes, meal plans, and lifestyle tips outlined in "Hashimoto's Diet for Beginners: A Cookbook with 100 Quick, Easy, and Delicious Recipes for Thyroid Healing and a 30-Day Meal Plan," you can take proactive steps towards optimizing your health and well-being.

For inquiries, assistance, or recipe support, please contact: [Sarah Grace Morgan]

mailto:wellnesswritingsarah@gmail.com

Thank you for choosing "Hashimoto's Diet for Beginners: A Cookbook with 100 Quick, Easy, and Delicious Recipes for Healing Thyroid and a 30-Day Meal Plan" by Sarah Grace Morgan. We hope you enjoy the nutritious and flavorful meals!

Your support means the world to me. If you found the book helpful and inspiring, I kindly ask for a review on Amazon or your favorite bookstore.

Your feedback will help others discover the benefits of Hashimoto's diet. I appreciate your time and input. Happy cooking and may your journey to health and wellness continue to thrive!

Made in the USA
Las Vegas, NV
22 July 2023